Dr. Tim's Moment Of Clarity readers' comments:

"Of all the great ideas/thoughts you have written over the last years, the last three paragraphs nearly moved me to tears." Tom B.

"This makes so much sense no politician will touch it." Roger B.

"Brilliant commentary, Tim." Renee M.

"Quickly becoming one of my faves!" T.C.

"Finally someone with some common sense". Benny B.

"As right as right can be". Gerard B.

"Amen!" Richard B.

"You said it better than I have ever seen it said." Abigail R.

"Brilliant as usual." Lisa F.

"I almost peed myself I was laughing so hard." Daniel B.

"Just Brilliant! Thank you for making my week!" Greg B.

"Seriously funny!" Alena H.

"Pure genius!" Anon

"Love, love, love, this Tim!" Stefanie S.

"Now THIS should be read and discussed in schools." Sharon

"I can not believe how you nailed it." Jacqui H.

"You inspire me!" Jena E.

CAPITALISTA!

FOREWORD
By Vicki McKenna

Tim Nerenz came on my radio program a few years back when he announced his "Tim, Not Tammy" campaign for Wisconsin's 2nd District congressional seat on the Libertarian Party ticket.

He said something so simple in his opening statement I almost missed the actual meaning. He said, "Liberty is the absence of government in choice; government is the absence of liberty in choice; and tyranny is the absence of choice in government."

So I asked myself this question: do I want more or less choice? The more choice I have, the less government; and the more government, the less choice. More choice: I decide. Less choice: government decides. And whom do I trust more - me, or government?

Well, given the abysmal state of affairs in Social Security, Medicare, Medicaid, welfare policy, education policy, energy policy, tax policy, and social engineering policy under the control of government, thanks, but I pick me. And I pick you. And so does Tim Nerenz.

I've long thought that someone had to write the "Freedom for Dummies" manual, but then I realized Milton Friedman already did it, as did our founding fathers. Well, Tim Nerenz tries again.

His is not the stuff of complicated math formulas, and high minded ethereal conceptualizations of liberty of the ivory tower-tweed jacket set with sets letters after their last names they all find useful to impress one another over white whine and cocktails (sorry, white WINE). Though he would easily hold his own among these preening sophists, HIS is the stuff of the world of the real working man.

You know that guy, the one everyone claims to care about, but no one can define. The guy who works long hours, doesn't take a break till he's finished his work, breaks a sweat, makes a payroll, pays his taxes? Yeah, him. Work. Ownership. Choice. Freedom. Because that's who Tim Nerenz is. That's how Tim Nerenz rolls.

CAPITALISTA!

What you'll learn in these pages is that not a one of these things (work, ownership, choice, freedom) can be separated from the others. They simply go together like bratwurst and beer. All the elements that make freedom grand and great in the abstract are the same things that make it work as a model for prosperity and make it work as a model for life.

But you don't have to fret that this will be a dull, plodding expose of the trappings of liberal tyranny and a marginal, academic defense of freedom. You see, Tim Nerenz thinks freedom is FUN. By the time you're done with "Capitalista!", so will you.

So just decide, right now: who owns you.

If you say "I own me", then read on in "Capitalista!". The writings here cover a span of time when the economic and political upheavals since 2008 called into question our ability to even ask that question. For the first time in generations, the question mattered. How we answer it is everything. How will we choose to answer? It is not a question to answer lightly, and one we cannot afford to get wrong. One path leads to liberation, the other to certain tyranny.

And so I stand with Tim Nerenz, raised fist over my head, wearing my Gadsden flag t-shirt, clutching my Ayn Rand and Pocket Constitution and shouting from the rooftops:

CAPTIALISTA! CAPITALISTA! SOY CAPITALISTA!

Viva la liberacion!

Vicki McKenna

AUTHOR'S INTRODUCTION

Liberals want government to impose social justice; conservatives want government to uphold traditional values; and libertarians just want government to leave us alone. It's a little more complicated than that, but not much.

This book, *Capitalista!*, is a collection of fan-favorite essays from my libertarian blog "Dr. Tim's Moment of Clarity" which is found on my website www.timnerenz.com.

My purpose in writing is to make libertarian ideas accessible to ordinary people; to make principled arguments in plain language, trusting the reader to sort out the common sense from the nonsense and reach their own conclusions.

I make no apologies for being a raving, radical *Capitalisa*. Free enterprise is the only economic system compatible with the ideal of self-sovereignty. Capitalism, for all its faults, has lifted more people out of poverty than any other "ism" put to the test in all of the centuries of human history. If history was taught honestly, there would be no need for me or anyone else to defend it. If.

Most of the criticism of profits comes from people who have never had to turn one. Most of the carping about worker rights comes from people who have never had to make a payroll. Most of the railing against corporations comes from people who never worked in one, let alone been responsible for its survival.

Truth is, most of the critics of capitalism don't have any idea what they are talking about. They mindlessly repeat the tired and boring talking points of others who didn't know what they are talking about, either.

Most practicing capitalists don't have the time or the desire to correct the hopelessly ignorant or debate those unacquainted with basic economic principles – socialists, unionists, statists, crony-capitalists, and liberals whose only answer to every problem is more government. I made time. Hope you like the book.

Acknowledgements

Everything starts with my wife Joanne, who encouraged me to start writing when I was a candidate for U.S. Congress a couple years ago. I love her for that, plus all the other things.

Linda Werth manages the posting of my blog to the national websites that carry it, making it accessible to millions of members of liberty groups around the world. I am grateful to Linda for doing all the stuff that gets the work out there.

Thanks to Mark Block, who introduced me to a boatload of interesting people: John Stossel, Judge Andrew Napolitano, Herman Cain, Stephen Moore, John Fund, Vicki McKenna, Grover Norquist, Dick Morris, Gen. Peter Pace, Dr. Arthur Laffer, and Michael Reagan, to name a few.

The first two speaking invitations I received as a Libertarian candidate were from the Rock River Patriots and Rick and Rudy Eckert at Olympia Resort. That took some guts, and I can't thank you guys enough.

And finally to Vicki McKenna, Wisconsin radio icon and fellow traveler in the liberty movement. Most of Vicki's fans would be thrilled with an autograph; I got a book foreword. How cool is that?

CAPITALISTA!

A COLLECTION OF LIBERTARIAN ESSAYS

TIM NERENZ, Ph.D.

TABLE OF CONTENTS

Capitalista!

It is fitting that Wisconsin, birthplace of socialist progressivism in this nation, is the epicenter of the revolution that will bring about its demise.

For a century, the Progressive's fundamental assertion that government exists to correct socio-economic disparity has been blindly accepted by both Democrats and Republicans alike, who differ primarily in their choice of targets for the slathering of massive amounts of somebody else's money.

The problem, of course, is that this fundamental assertion is wrong. Socio-economic disparity is not curable injustice, and even if it were, Government does not exist to cure; in America it only exists to protect individual rights.

That is the plain meaning and purpose of our Constitution; it is the idea that differentiates us from all other nations and made us exceptional. We have become less different and less exceptional with each step our socialist statists have pushed us away from our founding principles.

In the late 19th century, German socialists' concept of the welfare state found its way to their American cousins in Wisconsin. The progressive ideal was like a young Brett Favre – new, different, brash, energetic, exiting, a bit unconventional, but thrilling nonetheless. Back then, it made Wisconsin feel important.

A century later, socialist progressivism is still like him - old and tired, overpaid and overrated, self-absorbed and morally corrupted, a revered old memory haunting a dysfunctional body long past its prime. Now, it only makes Wisconsin's public unions feel important.

Wisconsin, of all places, should have no fear about leaving the old guard behind and moving forward with the next thing. Seniority and tenure did not bring the Lombardi trophy back home in February; that took young leadership willing to put the good of the team ahead of coddling a greybeard who had come to imagine he ran the joint. It took the courage to do the right thing.

CAPITALISTA!

Backward Wisconsin! can be seen on the Capitol square protests in Madison; yelling, threatening, vandalism, intimidation, extortion, vulgarity – an orgy of contrived victimhood from the people who made victimhood and its remedy one of the state's leading industries. But *Forward Wisconsin!* can also be seen on the Capitol square – once the weather turns nice and Farmers' Market begins on weekends.

On Farmers' Market Saturdays, a miracle happens in the People's Republic of Madison: all those hard-core socialists become raving capitalists. While the Capitol building – the symbol of government – stands by in laissez-faire stony silence, tens of thousands of people "spread the wealth around" all by themselves!

Without being coerced by law, regulation, or injunction from a county judge, the sandal people all circle counter-clockwise past hundreds and hundreds of produce stands while producers charge what they wish and consumers pay what they wish. No politically-appointed Czar makes up rules to follow, yet everybody is smiling and happy. Come down to the Capitol on a Saturday and see what capitalism looks like.

Nobody is screaming except the kettle corn cowboy, no drums are beating except for a beatnik bongo here or there, and nobody is drawing Hitler moustaches on pictures of vendors who asked them to buy their own asparagus. Jesse Jackson does not fly in on a private jet to mumble something that rhymes with broccoli. No forms, EEOC audits, diversity training, FDA inspectors - just people doing business with people.

That's capitalism. On Saturdays at the Farmers' Market, those lovable Madison moonbats do not expect some logger from Pence to buy them food insurance so they can get all the squash they want for free. Get 'em out of their cubicles and they get it – maybe fresh air is the ticket.

They look, they linger, they barter, they buy, or they walk away and wait for the vendor in the tie-died shirt to cave. On Saturdays, the sandal people do not pool all their purchases and sort out equal shares for everyone in town, and they do not vilify

---

the farmer who sold the most and went home richer than the rest.

Why is it so hard for them to imagine a world where it is Farmers' Market everywhere all the time? Is it impossible to fathom that people can do business with people for all the other millions of products and services that are exchanged on a daily basis without the need for government intervention at every turn? What is so unique about turnips?

Is it inconceivable that other people might get rich exactly the same way that top farmer does – by working harder and producing more of what people want to buy?

People do business with people - that is the first lesson we teach our young people coming into business out of school. Commerce occurs at a particular moment of exchange when one person chooses to buy what another person chooses to sell. That voluntary exchange is what adds value, creates wealth, and increases prosperity.

Government is not in the room at that magic moment; it adds no value. Its only useful role – the one assigned to it by our Constitution - is to protect the sanctity of the exchange; to defend property rights, enforce contracts through courts, bust monopolies, provide infrastructure, and give us sound money so we don't need a whole suitcase of Federal Reserve Notes to buy a strawberry at next year's Farmers' Market.

A century of unwise progressive government economic interventions have turned much of our capitalist system into a crippled, dysfunctional mess that protects failure and punishes success. General Motors was once the poster kid for American capitalism; and sadly enough, it still is.

If GM is what passes for capitalism these days, then call me something else: maybe X-treme capitalist, or Shi'ite Capitalist, or how about *Capitalista!* That's it, *Capitalista!* – combat boots, camo fatigues, beret cocked to one side, and fist in the air clutching a big wad of cash. *Soy Capitalista!*

You don't need a Ph.D. in economics or commerce to understand the simple genius of free market capitalism. Go to any farmers' market, flea market, gun show, garage sale, get on E-bay; personally, I recommend taking in a *Mercado* in any Latin American country. Supply and demand, price elasticity, substitution effect, marginal utility – it's all being taught without the tedium of reading textbooks.

And observe what you don't see - government. Nobody is banning things that you want to buy, forcing you to buy things you don't want, taxing one thing and subsidizing another, and making you buy things for someone else. You decide what you want to purchase at what price you are willing to pay with your own money. Every man for himself - what a revolutionary idea.

And who is it that says that *every man for himself* is a greedy and immoral creed? That would be the sandal people - socialist progressives on government payrolls whose idea of enlightened economic justice is *every man for me.*

We *Capitalistas* don't have time to waste debating self-absorbed fools unacquainted economic principles; there are sales to close, profits to make, and jobs to create. And besides, the moral argument for free enterprise was won at "free".

Viva La Revolución!

Mommy Dearest

The libertarian argument for less government is made each and every day for us by the silly things that government does. The more distant the level of government, the dumber those things are. That is the founding principle behind the United Nations; some things are just too stupid for one country to do by itself.

This year's U.N. float in the Stupid Parade is a proposed treaty which would recognize the earth as a living thing with rights equal to humans – Mother Earth. This is the sort of notion that distinguishes blithering idiots from the non-blithering generic kind of idiots.

The language will be patterned after Bolivia's Law of The Rights Of Mother Earth, recently enacted by its socialist President Evo Morales. That Bolivian law establishes a Ministry of Mother Earth and provides an Ombudsman to listen to her complaints. No, seriously, it does. I honestly can't decide which U.N. idea is goofier: ascribing human rights to a planet or emulating Bolivia.

For those unfamiliar, Bolivia is the poorest nation in the Western Hemisphere. Not coincidently, its President Morales has imposed the most anti-capitalist and anti-corporate policies in the Americas. While neighbors Peru, Colombia, and Brazil are prospering by developing their resources, embracing industry, and attracting foreign investment, Morales is digging himself a deeper hole with socialist insanity and superstitious hoodoo like his Mother Earth Law.

In the United States, the Mother Earth argument has already been used to block economic development, particularly in natural resource industries like mining, timber harvesting, water, and oil and gas exploration. The tortured reasoning goes that nature is a person, too, and every activity of man injures her. Get ready for a full dose of it as the mine project in northern Wisconsin moves forward towards permitting.

The word selection is important to the earthers – she is always feminine, and always victimized by men. There is no movement for White Dude Earth, the uncaring rich old bastard who rains on Gay Pride parades and hoards his minerals and water underground where poor people can't get at them. No, the earth-person of the United Nations and communist environmental extremists has mommy bits, doesn't shave her legs, hates guns, and thinks teachers are underpaid.

The idea of an inanimate object having human rights is proof that if you think long enough, you can make yourself believe anything. To state the obvious, human rights are the stuff of individual humans. Not collective humans, not their pets, not the Simpsons, farm animals, crops, trees, wind, planets, the universe, dead things, words, rocks, or cheese hats made of plastic.

Even if there were such a thing, Mother Earth would not be kindly June Cleaver, cleaning the oven in heels and pearls and offering up fresh cookies to Wally and Eddie Haskell after track practice. She would be Mommy Dearest, a raging Joan Crawford marinated in alcohol and stoked on amphetamines, cussing us out and beating us senseless with coat hangers. What comes to mind when you think back to that 24" inch blizzard this winter – "thanks, Mom"? Probably not.

Just to humor the UN whack jobs, let's say that Mother Earth does have rights; well then she has responsibilities, too. Here Mumsie – pay the $8 billion tab for Katrina; it's already a couple years past due and headed for collections. Tsunami, floods, blizzards, droughts, earthquakes, volcanoes – you went on quite a rampage recently, there, sister; hope you have paid up insurance and a good lawyer.

The earthers, I'm sure, would say that all those horrible natural disasters are the punishment we should expect for being loathsome humans. Oh, yeah? What did the dinosaurs do to deserve extinction, leave massive reptilian finger prints on the coffee table? Graze with their mouths open? And how do you know what she thinks - did she tell you? Do you two speak Earth when you chat? Ask her if this Global Warming thing was just a hot flash, now that it's over.

There is no arguing with the Mother Earth crowd – theirs is a religious conviction based on hatred of humans generally and human economic activity specifically. The only sure way to derail their Mother Earth movement is to tell them the Koch Brothers gave her a few bucks and watch them vibrate in place.

Earth Whore! Planet Bitch! Nature Slut! Misspelled signs calling her the K-word, Michael Moore cussing out vegans, Congresswoman Tammy Baldwin demanding Eric Holder's Justice Department put humanity in foster care until there is a recount – you get the picture. President Obama would appoint a commission to determine where her ass is so he could kick it. Sarah Palin would drop to #2 on the list of the left's most despised moms.

Clearly, the United Nations has too much time on its hands. Having secured world peace, eradicated hunger, lifted mankind out of poverty, vanquished disease, educated all the planet's children, and written thousands of sternly-worded letters to dictators, what is left to do?

Besides empower a new class of parasitic lawyers and a slew of mentally unbalanced Mother Earth activists to sue humanity on behalf of a plaintiff who can't file her own complaints because she is dumb as a stone. Not surprising, since she is a stone.

And speaking of lunatics, how in the world did we get to the brink of shutting down our own government without first defunding the United Nations? Democrats and Republicans agreed to cut $39 billion out of domestic spending but both thought it urgent that this bunch of foreign fruitloops maintain their lavish lifestyle on our dime? Is Rosetta Stone translation software co-owned by the teachers' union and the Ohio chamber of commerce or something?

Here is what we should do about the United Nations: cut them off, cut them loose, and when they throw a tantrum about it tell them to ask their Earth Mommy to increase their allowance and let them use her credit card.

PART ONE: RUN-UP to the 2010 ELECTIONS
August – November 2010

Liberty and Prosperity

This November's choice between capitalism and socialism is not about whether you are rich or poor right now; it is about which of those two you wish to be tomorrow.

The inescapable lesson of economic history is that free market economies make everyone unequally richer, while state-controlled economies make everyone equally poorer. Which do you prefer – rich or equal? Free people overwhelmingly choose rich, which is why socialism can only be imposed by force or fraud.

Nobel-winning economist F.A. Hayek's profound insight was that socialism fails because all of the information needed to make rational choices for millions of people can not possibly be known. Conversely, capitalism works because all of the information we need to make rational choices *is* known – it is known to us, and we make our own choices according to our own self-interest.

Self-interest is not immoral; it is simply the public interest reduced to its smallest indivisible component part. In fact, self-interest is the only kind of interest there is. If it were possible to establish a public interest by government decree, we would not need divorce lawyers. And if State power can not even bind two people who love each other, how could we expect it to herd 300 million strangers?

The simple answer is we can't, and we are proving Hayek's theorems daily. It has been nearly four years since the election of 2006 that gave control of Congress to Nancy Pelosi and Harry Reid. No one will confuse them with Ayn Rand and Milton Friedman; their agenda is anti-capitalist and socialistic, if not definitively socialist. The results speak for themselves: 15 million people have no jobs, the average work week for those who do has declined to 34.1 hours, property values have shrunk, the markets are still down, and the dollar has weakened. We are getting poorer.

People do not save, invest, and produce in order to benefit the State; they do so to benefit themselves and their families. That is why our economy has not, does not, *and will not* respond to the prompting of the President's socialist economic agenda or the deceptive pleadings of his minions. Federal Reserve Chairman Bernanke finally spoke the truth last month when he told Congress that it will be years before the jobless situation improves - *years.*

Chairman Bernanke is not clairvoyant; rather, he understands a basic economic principle: the bigger the rake, the less the take. Having learned nothing from their failures, our socialists in Congress plan to impose the largest tax increase in the history of the world this fall when they repeal the Bush tax reductions enacted almost a decade ago. This is the plan for reducing *their* deficit – to *increase* yours.

Think about the effect that just one of those tax increases – the inheritance tax – will have on job creation. The rate increases from 0% to 55%; children will have to sell the family business just to pay the death tax. Now, do you think this will encourage more people to start new family businesses? Congratulations! You and the Chairman of the Federal Reserve understand that people will not risk their life savings and work like a dog to bequeath their rewards to the IRS.

However, our President and his socialist colleagues in Congress don't get it. They are obsessed with their own jealous resentments and their brains are marinated in leftist economic gibberish.

Confiscating earnings from high earners does not make the poor richer anymore than cutting the heads off of tall people makes short people taller. All it does is increase government power and control over rich and poor alike, which is what the upcoming tax debate is really all about. It has been what all of the debates have been about for quite some time, now.

Recent polls show that 75% of Americans trust free markets, not government, to secure their prosperity. Less than 30% believe the President's economic stimulus plan has worked. Less than 20% approve of the job Congress is doing. Congress should listen to the People; we have it right, and they have it wrong. Any fool can see that now, unless they work in the media or teach in a University.

It is not complicated: reduce taxes, cut spending, shrink government, de-regulate markets, and let us live free and prosper – that is the answer to our economic problems, not higher taxes and bigger government.   Prosperity is not an entitlement program; it can not be legislated into being and delivered by the apparatus of the State. It is the product of free people pursuing their individual self-interest; engaging in voluntary economic cooperation and adding value in the marketplace.

Liberty is prosperity, and vice versa. Candidates who get this deserve your support in the upcoming elections, regardless of party affiliation or endorsement; candidates who don't deserve to be shelved, regardless of party affiliation or endorsement.

Want to save the nation? Find a candidate who gets it and help them win their campaign for liberty.

Welcome To Wisconsin

When President Obama returns to Wisconsin this month, you can have your picture taken with him for $10,000. I think I will bring a check for $1,427 to teach him how his proposed new tax rates will impact those of us who actually pay taxes.

First of all, let's assume he is a responsible retirement saver and is putting away 8% of his $10,000 earnings into a 401(k) - that is an $800 withholding that we will tax later. His Medicare tax on the balance is $267, Social Security tax is $1,150, and his federal income tax is $3,588 under his new top marginal rate.

His state income tax withholding is $1,023. Welcome to Wisconsin, Mr. President; now you know why people are leaving.

Wisconsin will not only tax this $10k, but also the pro-rated portion of his Presidential salary that he earns while breathing our air. We forgot to nail him in Racine last month, so I tacked two more days onto this bill. Don't complain, sir, or we will declare you a Wisconsin businesses and hit you with combined reporting – then we can tax the royalties from your book sales in Paraguay. Talk to the hand.

So that leaves the President with take home pay of only $3,172. Welcome to the tea party, brother; maybe now you know why we are all wee-weed up.

But we're not done with the carnage yet; the President is imposing a 55% inheritance tax this year. If, God forbid, he should die before he can cash my picture-posing-paycheck, the new Obama death tax would grab another $1,745.

Leaving only $1,427 for little Malia Ann and Sasha. Welcome to the Libertarian Party, girls; there's more to it than just low taxes, but you have to be a little older for that other stuff.

Oh, wait..... That photographer got paid, didn't he? The IRS might just decide he was acting "substantially as an employee", and unless the President provided health insurance, the estate would owe that new $2,000 health care head tax that was "the right thing to do".

Now, the way Mr. Obama's poll numbers are trending these days, I might be the only guy to show up for the photo op, so his girls would have give back the $1,427 from my $10,000 and then cough up another $286.26 apiece from the money they earned doing their chores and putting their baby teeth under the pillow.

This is an outrage! I can't be a party to the looting of innocents; so on second thought, I think I will just pass on this Obama picture thing altogether and let those sweet little girls keep the money they earned.

Because, my dear liberal socialist Democrat friends, letting sweet little girls keep the money they earned is what cutting taxes, reducing spending, and limiting government is all about. For the children, like you always say.

Climate Change

For many years, the left has sought to deflect criticisms of its job-killing economic ideology with the false promise that government investment in green technology would create a renaissance in American manufacturing, as if more government could cure the injuries caused by too much government.

The problem with the socialists' "green jobs" theory is that the contrived incentives designed by academics, politicians, and speculators who are overtly hostile to industry can't overcome the adversarial regulatory, tax, and tort climate that drives capital investment and jobs out of this country.

Their puny temporary ladders won't get anyone over their enormous permanent fences.

Recent failures of several prominent "green" showcase projects – Evergreen Solar, SpectraWatt, Tulsa, to name just a few - demonstrate the obvious point that well-intentioned environmentalists can not seem to grasp: the laws of economics, just like the laws of physics, cannot be amended to fit our hopes, beliefs, and desires.

The foundry does not know whether its castings will be used to make windmills or nuclear warheads. It only knows that the EPA is cutting off its energy supply, the NLRB wants to impose a union, new health care mandates increase its operating costs, their unemployment insurance rates are going through the roof, and DOL raised their minimum wage.

If they can somehow survive the fishing expeditions of OSHA, ADA, EEOC, and IRS auditors, they get to take on the harassment of state and local bureaucracies and a network of collaborating environmental activists hell-bent on shutting them down. If they are still standing, a fleet of slip-n-trip lawyers awaits, hoping to hit the lottery with a non-stop barrage of spurious lawsuits and class-action shakedowns.

If you are looking for climate change that will improve our standard of living, start with changing the hostile business climate that has driven industry after industry off-shore, unilaterally surrendered our energy independence, and destroyed our economic base. The green jobs are being created in China for the same reason all the other jobs are being created in China – the left won't let us make things here.

But the folks who make those puny temporary ladders are living large. Somebody has to write the bills that start the money flowing, somebody has to write the grants asking for the handouts, somebody must manage the subsidies to make sure they are all being properly peed away, somebody must lobby for more spending, somebody must market the boondoggles, somebody must drive Al Gore's limousine, light T-Boone Pickens' cigars, and buy Bill Gates' software to blog about climate change.

And don't forget conferences – lots and lots of conferences – and research – can't have a proper gluttonous orgy at the public trough without research. How did that song go? Look for...the union la-bel....guess what strings are attached to the construction of the alternative energy infrastructure that goes belly up a few years after it is built, even with operating subsidies that run into the billions.

There's your green jobs; some union patronage and an expansion of the public payroll dole whose only long-term return on our green investment will be even higher pension liabilities we can't pay for.

The first solar panel was patented in 1888; the first wind turbine factory was built in 1891; bio-fuels preceded oil as a source for combustion engines. If these were economically viable energy sources, the private sector would have developed and deployed them to scale decades ago. Fact is, the massive amounts of energy it takes to make and move the things that 310 million Americans want can not be produced by renewable sources; only by the three F's – fossil, fission, and fusion.

Environmentalists argue that fossil fuels are also heavily subsidized; that the cost of harm to the commons – pollution of the air and water and consequences of CO_2 emissions – are not born by the energy producers, who are viewed as profiteering free riders. Their complaints extend to mining, agriculture, manufacturing, transportation, virtually every goods-producing field of endeavor. It is a valid argument as far as it goes, but it does not go far enough.

Imagine yourself sitting in an intensive care unit, praying for your severely injured child to survive the night. Look around: everything made of plastic came from a barrel of oil. Everything made of metal or glass was mined. Every woven good was made in factories that run on fossil fuel energy. Every light, pump, monitor, and communications device is consuming energy and emitting carbon as it works to save her life. And every single thing in that room, including your precious little girl and the doctors and nurses who will deliver God's answer to your prayers, was transported there in a vehicle powered by an internal combustion engine. The only reason any of those things came into existence is because capitalists made money on them.

Was their profit excessive? Is the tragedy of the commons more important than the tragedy of human potential unnecessarily denied? Not if it is my little girl.

Maurice Strong, head of the 1992 Earth Summit in Rio de Janeiro and until recently, Executive Officer for Reform in the U.N. Secretary General's office, put the climate change industry's cards on the table, when he wrote, "Isn't the only hope for the planet that the industrialized nations collapse? Isn't it our responsibility to bring that about?"

No, Mr. Strong, it isn't, you self-absorbed asshole. Our responsibility is to insure that liberty is restored in this nation, so that little girls and boys grow up and thrive in a land of opportunity, freedom, and prosperity. The only hope for the planet is that guys like you have the right to freely speak your mind, but no power to impose your idiotic notions onto others.

The planet will be saved when human potential is liberated from the burden of government-imposed mediocrity, when education displaces indoctrination in government-monopoly schools, and when free market capitalism forces socialist state crony-corporatism into hasty retreat.

Less government means more real jobs; and real jobs come in all colors – including green. We have wasted enough time on the wrong answer, and we need to get government out of the way of market solutions that will solve our most urgent problems.

About Race

Here is one thing I have learned over 35 years in business: winners do not think of themselves as white or black, male or female, gay or straight, disabled or able. Here is another: losers are obsessed with such things.

That is what's most wrong with liberals' pre-occupation with race, gender, and class – they are teaching another generation of young people to think like losers, talk like losers, and act like losers. When these young people grow up to be losers, it will be held up as evidence of more racism and sexism, and we will be asked to subsidize the victimhood industry into perpetuity.

In the private sector, we have no time for such self-indulgent foolishness.

We are rewarded and punished for our decisions and actions by the market - a market that is color-blind and gender-neutral. Its judgments are swift and final; our choice is to please it or disappear. We win or we lose; it is a beautiful thing – pure. No wonder free markets terrify people who expect a hug for simply showing up.

What matters in business are competence, confidence, character, and trust. These are not traits bestowed upon any specific race or gender; they are leadership characteristics that are found in *individual persons*. Winners have developed these characteristics in themselves, while losers have not.

Winners act and learn, while losers hope and blame. Losers hope for good things to happen to them, rather than making good things happen. They blame others for their circumstances, and exaggerate every slight and injustice, real or imagined.

In business, we teach our young leaders to recognize winners and losers by the language they use. Losers will announce themselves to the world with the "three F's": – it's not Fair, it's not my Fault, and it's not mine to Fix.

Waiting for someone else to cure one's circumstance is the loser's signature move.

We should not be afraid to speak plainly about these matters. Race is a cop-out. Gender is a cop-out. Orientation is a cop-out. Disability is a cop-out.

We are what we are, and none of us chose it; recognizing how our DNA configured us at birth is as much thought as these subjects deserve. What is important is who we have become, what we have made of ourselves. The making of a self is an individual pursuit.

Over the past 35 years, I have worked with, worked for, supervised, promoted, hired, and dismissed people of every age, race, gender, orientation, and physical ability. The winners win and the losers lose, without regard to their skin color or reproductive equipment. It has everything to do with what they have made of themselves, and how well they apply themselves to the job at hand.

And I will also say this: over those 35 years, I have witnessed more corruption, intolerance, harassment, favoritism, and overtly racist and sexist acts from the government employees who regulate us than I have from those of us in the private sector who supposedly need to be regulated. Here's the difference: in the private sector we fire our dipsticks, we don't promote them to GS13 and send them to a class.

I know many successful black, Hispanic, gay, and disabled men and women; I enjoy being in their company, working with them, competing against or cooperating with them as the case may be.

We don't talk about their EEO status; we talk about their accomplishments, values, family, faith, philosophy, relationships, strategies, and dreams for the future. Their dreams come true because the refuse to be defined by their skin or their genitalia. They refuse to be defined, period; they define themselves.

And I also know plenty of pathetic white male losers that blame their failure on preferences given to blacks, Hispanics, females, disabled, or veterans by government. You want to have a dialog on race and gender? That is all they talk about. Their preoccupation condemns them to a life of perpetual irrelevance just as surely as it does the minority teen whose head has been filled with the lie that she can't succeed without government benevolence.

The difference between the first (winners) and second (losers) set of acquaintances is not the color of their ears, or the loops that adorn them, or which side hosts the piercing. The difference is what is going on *between* those ears.

Each of us has a brain of our own, a heart of our own, and our Creator's emancipating endowment of free will. We are not Leggo pieces to be sorted into neat piles by color and shape so that social engineers can more easily construct a society that pleases them.

Rev. Jesse Jackson had it exactly right with "I am somebody"; singular, not plural. It should all just stop right there.

Smarter Than A 20ᵗʰ Grader

The magic number is $50,000 – the median compensation rate in the private sector. The math is simple: for every $50,000 of cost laid on business by government, one job must be cut.

Government burdens businesses in three ways: taxes, mandates, and regulations. Ultimately, these costs are passed to consumers in the form of increased prices; but in the short run, increased government burden must be offset with cost reductions elsewhere in the firm, and elsewhere these days almost always means job cuts.

Who is surprised that businesses are cutting jobs again? Are taxes going up or down? Are regulations being added or removed? Are mandates increasing or decreasing? The U.S. Chamber of Commerce estimates the 20 new mandates in the Health Care Reform Bill will increase employers' benefit costs by 20% to 60%. What does that mean for jobs? Let's do the math.

For a firm with 1,000 employees, a 20% increase could mean more than $1 million in additional benefit costs. Divide by our magic number of $50,000 and you have 20 jobs that will be cut as a result of HCR. That doesn't seem like very many until you realize there are 80 million workers whose employers are learning the details of ObamaCare this "recovery summer" and buzz-killing Joe Biden's victory lap. 484,000 Americans lost their jobs last *week*.

Government economists don't use the magic number; they forecast employment changes using computer models that are vastly more intricate and complicated – and wrong. This is why we constantly read news stories about economists being surprised at the dismal jobs numbers month after month. Businesspeople are only surprised that the economists are surprised.

The magic number works for new government spending too, as funds for public sector programs are taken from the private sector. Last week Congress passed a $26 billion bailout of states to "save" 160,000 government jobs. That is $162,000 per government job "saved". How many private sector jobs will it cost to "save" them? You know the magic number – do the math. Plus one minus three is a net two jobs lost, so get ready to read about the President's economists being surprised again.

Fortunately, the knife cuts both ways - for every $50,000 of government burden *removed* from business, one new job will be *added* in the private sector. President Kennedy knew this, President Reagan knew this, Prime Minister Thatcher knew this, and the American people know this; a recent Rasmussen poll showed that 2/3 of us think Obama's economic policies have us headed in the *wrong* direction.

Want to solve the jobs crisis? Use the magic number. Lighten the load on business by $500 billion – we would create 10 million jobs and drop the unemployment rate below 4%. Cut taxes, repeal mandates, and de-regulate; start by eliminating the corporate income tax, and try to avoid getting trampled by the millions of people going back to work. It will be a beautiful thing.

And when that happens, the President's Keynesian economists will once again be dazed and confused; according to their models, this shouldn't work. Reason enough to do it - these nimrods have been wrong about *everything.* They are giving us 20th graders a bad name.

Mr. Obama's economic "Dream Team" has spent trillions after billions on one blunder after another that have only made things worse. Biden quit trying to spin it; Romer simply quit. Last Tuesday's headline, "Dems Pass $26 Billion Jobs Bill" was followed by Wednesday's, "Stocks Fall Sharply As Investor Gloom Grows." Ouch.

Why did investor gloom grow? Think of the economy as a family of four children: three of them have paper routes, pick strawberries, run lemonade stands, shovel snow, mow lawns – they earn their own money and exchange with each other to build wealth.

Then there is the fourth kid – he gets an allowance with money taken from the earnings of the first three. He spends all of his allowance on gifts for his friends, and then he borrows 60% more to buy even more gifts for his friends, racking up debt that the first three children must pay off.

When that fourth kid's allowance is increased by $26 billion, do you think the other three children will be happy or gloomy? Will they rush out and hire some neighbor kids or cut a few of their current helpers to come up with the $26 billion?

Congratulations, you are smarter than a 20th grader.

Pelosi University

It didn't take them as long as I thought - less than four months after nationalizing the student loan industry, the Department of Education is now moving to cut off funding to for-profit private schools.

In July, DOE proposed new rules that would assess how well post-secondary for-profits prepare students for "gainful employment" and deny student loan funding for schools that don't measure up (WSJ, August 17).

The new rules would only apply only to for-profit institutions and vocational programs of non-profits. Government schools are, naturally, exempted.

Now why would the government only go after schools that earn profits for stockholders and employ non-tenured instructors? Why does a frog croak? Who is John Galt? Socialists go after capitalists – its what they do.

The Democratic Socialists of America (DSA) list a "right" to a free *public* education in their 21st century Bill of Rights, making this demand on government: "the institutions of tenure and faculty-shared governance must be defended because they are integral to the liberating education we seek, and the "business model" of the university must be resisted."

Personally, I find it hard to believe that when our Creator decided to endow us with unalienable rights that He had tenure and faculty-shared governance on His mind. But can you think of any better way to "resist the business model" than to first nationalize the student loan industry and then pull student loan funding to all of the for-profit institutions? Nancy's way was ruthlessly efficient, with the emphasis on *ruthless*.

As you recall, nationalizing the student loan industry was an 11th hour naked power grab attached to the all-day-sucker of a naked power grab that was Nancy Pelosi's Health Care Reform. At the time, I suggested the purpose was to cut off loans to institutions who dared to challenge the dogma of the entrenched socialist academy.

The E.D. report that calls for killing off the for-profit schools does not define what "gainful employment" means; one can only guess that occupying a cube at the Department of Education with your integrated culture studies major from Berkley would certainly count, but the absence of clarity on this subject is irrelevant.

Because they don't propose to even assess the employment status of alumni in their evaluation of "employment readiness". They plan to strip a school's funding based solely on the rate of non-repayment of student loans. Schools who have asked for an explanation of the E.D.'s methodology of calculating non-payment rates have been stonewalled.

Let's just cut to the chase. The for-profit University of Phoenix has been beating the crap out of public universities for years, and the socialists in academia are all wee-weed up about it, to steal a phrase.

Over 400,000 grown men and women choose of their own volition to attend Phoenix classes via distance, instead of sitting in a class listening to some 23 year old TA tell you what some 28 year-old Ph.D. decided you should know about something a 40 year-old Ph.D. wrote about something a 60 year-old Ph.D. said 30 years ago.

These students borrow the money for tuition of their own volition. Banks loaned it to them of their own volition – or did before Obama put the Chavez on them. Course instructors teach in the for-profits of their own volition. Half a dozen competitors have adopted this business model of their own volition.

That is way too much volition, and our American socialists *hate* volition. It is that simple;

This has nothing to do with the quality of education. If that was the goal of the Department of Education, it would abolish itself and leave a poorly spelled suicide note behind. This has to everything to do with destroying capitalism, free enterprise, and liberty. We need to face up to the unimaginable truth that our most dangerous enemies are on the public payroll.

CAPITALISTA!

Our only saving grace is that E.D. are government workers and don't get much done in the occasional working hours that punctuate their numerous breaks and countless days off.

Friends, if you love liberty, go online to the website of Democratic Socialists of America: www.dsausa.org/dsa.html and force yourself to stare right down the barrel of the most clear and present danger to everything you hold dear. Read their Bill of so-called Rights and tell me what is different from the Obama/Pelosi/Baldwin agenda that is being enacted into law right before our disbelieving eyes.

Then go find yourself a candidate willing to call them by their name. Give whatever you can, and do whatever you must, to get a liberty candidate elected this November.

Or be prepared to send your child to Pelosi University.

Smokin'

Last weekend, we went to one of our favorite tavern-burger joints for the first time since Wisconsin's smoking ban went into effect. No ashtrays, no smoke...and no customers.   Nice going, do-gooders.

This was a biker bar, past tense. It is an empty bar now – soon to be a closed-down bar unless there is a federal bailout in the works for dives. It wasn't the kind of place you would walk into by mistake, not a place to take your kids.

Nobody was inadvertently exposed to second-hand smoke there. It was dependably loud and nasty and smoky; every patron and employee walked in there of their own free will. The Joe Camel sign on the door was 2 feet high. I can't repeat what the other signs say.

The regulars perched on their customary stools; drinking beer and smoking cigarettes, telling jokes, telling lies, and ogling the Harley girls who came in dressed like they tell their teenager daughters not to.

Retirees and veterans, mostly; old guys who walked down from the neighborhood to watch a game or watch a race or just watch a well-pierced barmaid with the mouth of a Teamster bend over to grab another beer from the cooler. This was not the Overture Center.

Would it have killed you to leave these people alone?

We just went there occasionally for the best steak sandwich on the planet.   Sometimes we took our 80-something moms and aunts there for lunch after church.   No one hassled us, even though we were dressed inappropriately in our Sunday duds. We coexisted, just like the bumper sticker says to. It was diversity without the forms, legislation, trainer, and fines. Gone now.

Our modern-day health fascists wouldn't dream of walking into that joint before or after the ban, so they have gained nothing but the self-righteous satisfaction of depriving someone else their liberty and property. Here's a suggestion if any are reading this:

pull that stick out and beat yourself with it the next time you feel an overwhelming urge to punish someone you don't like. Leave the rest of us alone.

Smoking-ban advocates insisted that the hospitality industry would boom afterwards, when hoards of non-smokers would come out to frequent the newly liberated smoke-free establishments. See for yourself how that is working out – take a drive up north on Hwy 13 or 45 and tell me how many of those tavern parking lots are full and how many are empty.

I've heard the argument; the bar owners' property rights and smokers' personal liberty are small sacrifices for the greater good of society. Wrong. Liberty lost is *never* good for society; in the words of John Stuart Mill: "the danger which threatens human nature is not excess but deficiency of personal impulses and preferences."

You will never discover your own true nature if you are denied the diversity of choices that requires you to form one.

I don't smoke – quit several years ago of my own volition. Recently an ad for Kools on sale at $67 a carton caught my eye – I'm told they are nearly $100 a carton in New York. That is more than a day's wages for the working poor who do most of the smoking in this country; a weekly smoking tax that is greater than the cost of health insurance. No wonder so many are uninsured. Maybe they should have just fixed that.

And weren't we going to tax only the rich? When did the rich start smoking Kools? Do any white people smoke Kools? Clearly this is racially motivated and Nancy Pelosi should investigate the tea party. Where is the liberal outrage over the Kool tax? Where are Jesse and Al and Maxine and Barack? For that matter, where is the conservative outrage? Heck, where is the libertarian outrage? Silence.

This isn't about smoking; this is about liberty and individual sovereignty and the tyranny of the majority. Again, John Stuart Mill: "If all of mankind save one were of one opinion, they would be no more justified in silencing the one than he, if he had the power, were justified in silencing mankind."

One less Wisconsin business, one less business tax payer, a few less jobs, lower incomes for the commissioned vendors, one fewer choice for bikers and veterans and retirees and our moms, and cigarettes that cost more than dope. To repeat: nice going.

The Wisconsin smoking ban sacrificed Liberty on the altar of the public good, the false idol of our modern times. The public did not become any "gooder", but a little liberty died.

You Can Call Me Ray.....

Recently it was reported that 70 Members of Congress belonged to the Democratic Socialists of America. The sourcing was a bit dubious, but none of the "outed" legislators has denied the claim, either, so we'll go with it for now.

A check of the DSA website reveals a political philosophy that is plainly anti-American. They argue that Americans are wrong to "believe that their security results from personal responsibility and individual initiative." Can they make their hatred of liberty any plainer?

The DSA reject our Constitution's Bill of Rights, and seek to impose a collectivist substitute called the 21st Century Bill of Rights. I present it here with verbatim quotes from their own amplifications, along with an italicized rebuttal commentary which is, of course, my own.

Everyone has the right to a living wage job. "...government, at the federal, state or local level, will necessarily be the prime mover in creating jobs that meet the social needs of an advanced industrial society".

Wrong. Trusting government as the "prime mover" has left 15 million Americans without any job whatsoever.

Everyone has the right to a sufficient amount of nutritious and safe food. "The answer to this is federal funding...profit alone cannot be the standard for such a necessity."

Oh, please. Look at the shapes of the workers exiting any federal government building at quitting time and tell me you want those people deciding what you should eat.

Everyone has the right to affordable and safe housing. "The goal of affordable and safe shelter can be realized by government programs and subsidies with mandated targets and timetables. Then and only then..."

Hello? We tried this – it was called sub-prime lending and it broke the world, remember?

Everyone has a right to preventive, acute and long term health care. "...and we must legislate the financing mechanism consistent with this belief: single-payer national health insurance."

Relentless, like Chucky. Health care is the product of someone's labor. You have a right to buy it; you don't have a right to steal it.

Everyone has a right to free, high quality public education. "...the institutions of tenure and faculty-shared governance must be defended...and the "business model" of the university must be resisted."

You can't be serious. I'm pretty sure when the Creator was endowing us with our equal and unalienable rights, university tenure was not on His mind. But now we all know where these loopy ideas originate.

Everyone has the right to give and receive care. "The United States is unique among advanced democratic nations by making caring for one's loved ones primarily a private burden."

Are you guys smoking crack? The 90% of Americans who are not socialist wingnuts do not view caring for our loved ones as a burden; it is our greatest joy.

Everyone has the right to income security throughout their life. "The result is a society that moves towards its economic potential and an economic policy whose goals are for all of us to live "wisely, agreeably and well.""

Ok, how about Lindsay Lohan? I hear she is in a "transitional phase" – how much income does LiLo have a right to? Let's ask mom Dina what they would both find "wise, agreeable, and well" and then deduct it from Congressional pay.

Everyone has the right to leisure time. "The pursuit of profits by capitalists is in direct opposition to leisure time."

Alright, give me the pipe. Sure, let's just chuck Life, Liberty, and the Pursuit of Happiness, and go with Tenure, Early Pension, and

Time Off. This is what happens when government workers write the specs for Utopia.

Everyone has the right to a healthy environment. "Our posterity will inherit a healthy planet only if we end the profit-driven throwaway corporate economy..."

Excuse me, but the last time you socialists ended the profit-driven economy someplace, we got Chernobyl. Nobody washes a rental car, comrade.

Everyone has the right to associate in whatever organizational form they choose. "Only a major mobilization....could put enough spine in timid Democratic politicians to pass any substantive reform like EFCA."

You mean the right to associate in any organizational form that is a union or ACORN. What about my right to associate with tea partiers, libertarians, NRA members, non-unionized co-workers, stockholders, raw milk drinkers, smokers, drivers who don't want to pay your stupid train fare, talk-radio listeners, and people who feel like endorsing candidates on Facebook? I didn't think so.

Well, there you have it, my friends – that's the game plan. Not a peep about speech, religion, arms, privacy, property, states' rights, warrants, jury trials, or press freedom; in fact, there are no individual rights whatsoever - just a collective right to be a soulless and dependent ward of the State.

And can you show me the plank that President Obama or Speaker Pelosi would oppose? Can you name the goal you have not heard them plead in their own words? Whether or not there are 70 card-carrying DSA members in Congress is irrelevant; there are hundreds who gleefully carry the water every day.

I call them socialists because it is what they are; we should quit pretending otherwise.

Taxing and Spending

Some have questioned how President Obama paid for his Ivy League education; I wonder *why* he paid for it. If you can graduate from Columbia and Harvard without knowing the difference between taxing and spending, you should ask for your money back.

At his press conference last week, the President, for the umpteenth time, described leaving the existing tax rates alone as "spending". He said we had "better things to spend our money on" than not raising taxes.

Did he really say "our money"? Oh yes, he did. That's what they call your paycheck these days over at the White House; and you keeping what you earned is now considered foolish spending. The press corps – more refund-eligible Ivy League alumni who apparently majored in economic illiteracy and minored in Marx – did not call him on it.

Perhaps in the Obama household, Barack resisting his urge to steal Sasha's babysitting money is the same thing as Michelle buying a dozen pair of Jimmy Choos.

But for us rubes who grew up in small towns and worked our way through state schools, the distinction between not-stealing and spending is quite obvious. In fact, most of us figured out complicated things like taxes, spending, and the income gap long before we ever graduated from high school.

When we were 5 or 6, we shoveled snow for a nickel a sidewalk. The kids who shoveled a lot of sidewalks had a lot of money for candy. Those who did one or two and then went sledding didn't have as much. There's your income gap.

When we were 8, we got paper routes. Some kids took bigger routes, worked longer and carried the heavier bags, and we made more money than the kids who took the short routes and got done earlier to go play. There's your income gap.

When we were 10, we were big enough to pick rocks in the fields; we got paid by the rock. The longer and harder you worked the more you made. Some kids hit it all day long, and some kids were off riding their bikes by noon. There's your income gap.

Later in summer, we picked strawberries and got paid by the quart. If you could squat all day and had nimble fingers, you made serious cash. The 10 year-olds weren't very good at it, but by 14, we became skilled and (comparatively) wealthy. There's your income gap.

Where I grew up, we had a different idea about entitlements – if another kid tried to steal your stuff, you were entitled to bop him in the nose. And when his parents found out why he had a shiner, he was entitled to a heaping dose of shame and punishment at home. We didn't do lawyers or community organizers up North. I do not feel deprived.

At 15, we started to work in stores, run errands for contractors, or work for our dads who were tradesmen. Our first real paychecks, and the awful discovery of tax withholding. Did you say the Governor took it? Can I bop him in the nose? I already had a bad attitude before Civics and Econ class confirmed my worst suspicions of government.

Summers, after school, weekends – an introduction to time-and-a-half and punitive tax rates on those who worked longer and produced more. But the kids who went the extra mile still made a lot more than the kids who went swimming. There's your income gap again.

At 16 (well, close – I told you I'm from up North) you could drive, and that opened up a whole different world of income potential. When I could drive the painting contractor's car to pick up supplies, I got a big raise because I was more valuable to his crew. There's your income gap one more time.

And the income gap was important when you were a 16 year old guy up North. The guys who had worked and saved enough to get a car were cool, and girls went on dates with them. Those of us without cars were jealous; but we would never think of demanding they share their cars, their money, or their girls.

To be honest about it, if we could have "spread the wealth around" back then, we would have gone for the girls – to heck with the money and cars. Maybe that is coming next from Mr. Obama, and why not; if the insured owe health care benefits to the uninsured, don't married people owe conjugal benefits to unmarried people? Such is the morality of redistribution.

Now, if you think the slop just falls out of the sky into the trough, then you probably think that the biggest, fattest pigs must have got that way by abusing the skinny, timid ones. Those fat hogs must be punished and the slop must be redistributed by a benevolent and infallible farmer who cares that every little oinker gets a fair and equal portion.

This makes perfect sense if you are a barnyard animal - or a liberal Democrat.

But if you are a thinking human being who ever shoveled snow, picked rock, or worked weekends, you know that the slop does not fall from the sky; it is the product of someone's labor, and it belongs to the people who earned it. It is not *our* money; it is *their* money.

And, Mr. President, leaving it alone is not the same as spending it; those are two different things and you can expect a figurative bop on the nose in November for trying to take what doesn't belong to you. If you need money, get yourself a refund from Columbia and Harvard and leave the rest of us alone.

Just Tax The Rich

100 of us go to a tavern; the richest guy buys 42 tap beers, the next 9 buy 48 tap beers, 43 buy 10 tap beers, and 47 of us drink tap beers for free. In Wisconsin, we say "thank you" when someone else buys our beer; apparently in Chicago, they go find a community organizer and demand martinis.

The top 1% of income earners in this country - nice people like Oprah and Aaron Rodgers - make 28% of the income, yet they pay 42% of the income tax. 47% of Americans pay no income tax at all. Is that fair? President Obama doesn't think so; he thinks the rich should pay even more.

Why? Why should they pay more when almost half of us pay nothing? How is that fair? What do they get in exchange?

Will they have their own Bentley lanes on the Interstate Highways? Do they get extra protection if the Canadians invade? Will their trademarks and copyrights last twice as long as ours? No, we will offer them nothing; we will simply take their money because we want it.

Paul Krugman calls them "belligerent" for wanting to keep it. Is that what we have come to? When did we turn into a nation of looters? Why do we revile the strong and revere the weak? Why do we punish the champion and reward last place? It should be obvious to anyone that rich people consume less government services than poor people and pay most of the taxes. We should be grateful to have them; instead we demonize them.

It is stupid to hate rich people; all of us either work for rich people, or work for organizations funded by the taxes they pay or donations they make. We will not earn more when they keep less. Taxing them is a lose/lose proposition, which unfortunately has become this administration's signature move.

Wealth is neither moral nor immoral; it is simply the difference between what is produced and what is consumed over a lifetime. People who spend more than they earn become poorer, people who earn more than they spend become richer. With the obvious exceptions of crooks and shnooks, rich people only get that way by providing us with the things we want. Only a fool – or a jealous socialist - would want to punish someone for that.

And besides, who really suffers when we "tax the rich"? Your dentist is undoubtedly rich under Mr. Obama's fluid definition; so where will she get the money to pay the new taxes she will owe next year? You will give it to her one filling, crown, cleaning, and bridge at a time. Ditto your doctor, your car dealer, your landlord, your store keeper, your favorite artists, etc. It is trickle-up taxation.

Every time the hucksters in Congress pretend to sock it to "big fill-in-the-blank", it is the little fill-in-the-blanks who get screwed. You are already feeling the love this year if you tan, smoke, drink, drive, buy health insurance, or register a gun. A recent study showed that the President's proposed tax increases will cost $1,500 for a Wisconsin family of four making $60,000. That is not rich to me.

Another recent study revealed that White House appointees owe a combined $817,000 of back income taxes, and that government employees nationwide are over $2 billion in arrears. These tax cheats' average income is $120,000 per year and their health care benefits cost us $21,000. Isn't that just ducky?

We ask the parasites to recycle a few drops of blood to pay the unemployment benefits for the millions of people their bungling incompetence have made jobless, and they can't be bothered. Too busy calling *us* greedy. Too busy calling *us* selfish, uncaring, imperialist, exploiters, racist. Too busy telling *us* we don't pay our fair share; that we owe *them* more.

How about this for a tax policy: we don't pay another dime until all of the government deadbeats are current. Let those 16,000 new IRS agents squeeze the blood out of their own turnips before they come after the rest of us.

Increasing taxes on the wealthy will not stimulate economic growth and it will not eliminate the deficit. The President's tax increase on the richest 1% would only balance the budget for 9 days. In fact, we could take *all* of their earnings and it would still not pay for all of the spending in Washington. Reality check: we spend 50% more than we tax – 50%.

We have to spend less, not tax more, if we want our economy to recover.

They have figured this out in Germany, France, Greece, Britain, China, Venezuela, and even Cuba, where Castro will cut a million government jobs in the next year. He is down there channeling Chris Christie while our guys are high-fiving over the millions of cube jockeys they have added – the mind boggles.

My advice to candidates who want to get elected this year: name the programs, agencies, and departments you would eliminate and the amounts you would cut from the budgets of those which remain. The truth will not just set you free, it will send you to Washington and Madison.

Since You Asked

When the President's own supporters skewered him in his town hall meeting this week, he dodged their questions by challenging the tea party movement to name specific spending cuts we would approve. Ok, since you asked...

Abolish the Department of Education; leave the money in the hands of local school boards and parents.

Implement FairTax and abolish the IRS. Abolish the Agriculture Department, and privatize the FDA.

Abolish the Department of Energy, and maybe we would finally have enough of it.

Sell public lands to someone who will take care of them, abolish the Forest Service, and scrap the Department of Interior while you are at it. We already have 50 departments of the interior – they are called States.

End *all* corporate welfare – subsidies, tax credits, preferences, trade protections, price supports, grants, loan guarantees, and earmarks – and devolve personal welfare programs back to the states where they belong. If we quit rewarding lousy business managers and slackers we would have a lot fewer of both.

And how about reducing the number of Presidential vacations? I've been here 20 years and don't get that much time off. Or make Harry Reid's entourage drive Priuses (or is it Prii?).

Freeze federal pay scales until the average private sector catches up. Raise the retirement age for federal employees to 65 and graduate the scale to 70; eliminate double dip pensions. They might get mad and quit? Bonus!

The Labor Department exists to counter the clout of the Commerce Department, so eliminate them both. Dump all of the special trade negotiators; let people trade with people.

If we repeal ineffective drug laws, we have no need for the DEA or half the federal prisons.

Nix the NEA; people will buy art they like. Ditto NPR and the Kennedy Center.

Give veterans vouchers and dismantle the VA hospital system – we owe our veterans the best care available anywhere in the nation.

Abolish anything run by a Czar – anything.

Close all foreign military bases and eliminate all foreign aid. The Europeans can defend themselves if they are so dang healthy. Defend our borders and let South Korea worry about its own. We won in Iraq; now bring 'em home. Do the same in Afghanistan.

Pull out of the U.N, the IMF, WTO, WHO, the World Bank, and any other international organization run by world bureaucrats to benefit world bureaucrats.

Repeal Health Care Reform.

Don't spend whatever is left of the stimulus money. Get the TARP money back from the banksters. Cut off the water to AIG, Fannie and Freddie, and sell the public stake in the auto companies.

Drop that $8,000 bribe to buy one of those loopy GM Volts. Leave student loans to banks. End the Fed and privatize the money supply.

Don't replace any members of your economic team who quit and return to teaching. An empty chair is better than a credentialed fool and way cheaper. Oh, no - we're not done yet.

Round up every single department, agency, and program created to fight the War on Poverty and shut them down. Trillions of dollars have been thrown down that feel-good rat hole for half a century and poverty is higher than when we started.

Same for Affirmative Action; either it worked and we don't need it, or it didn't work and we don't need it. Either way, we don't need it.

And what's the deal with trains? Probably some kind of Freudian obsession of emasculated lefties. I'll buy your fare when you buy me a Harley – deal?

Abolish the ATF – we don't particularly care to fund agencies wholly devoted to constraining the Bill of Rights.

And if you are not going to use INS or ICE, cut them loose to find some private sector security work. Do we really need so many TSA's to disarm citizens of their gels and nail clippers? I think not.

How about we repeal the Patriot Act and leave us patriots alone.

Let's keep the Department of Justice, but not the parts of it that sue us or defend torture and indefinite detention now that Obama has control of the apparatus.

And you can cut out half of the research grants to your university buddies – welfare for Ph.D.s who can't teach.

That leaves Social Security and Medicare. Medicare is easy; give people the $11,000 that government spends to insure them and let them choose their own – cut out the middle man. Social Security is not so difficult either; give people the option of either staying in the current system or pulling out what they have contributed and funding their own retirement savings accounts. Transition both entitlements completely to personal account ownership over a 25 year period. Yes, we can.

And give people the option of working past 65 and keeping every penny they earn; that's right, zero taxes of any kind if you keep working and put off your benefit draw. The savings in deferred benefit payments would be enough to salvage social security, which is more than can be said for the accounting gimmicks proposed by either establishment Party.

I know it's a small thing, but how about we fire the guy who names laws. Taking our liberties away with legislation so awful it has to be disguised as "Protect Puppies and Orphans from All Harm Act" is not just juvenile, it's offensive. And if government wasn't so reliably offensive, we would not need a tea party movement.

There you go, Mr. President – roughly 70% of federal spending eliminated and plenty left over to perform the 17 essential functions of government authorized by the Constitution. Too radical? Did you expect a Libertarian to follow a road map?

The tea party is a movement, not a mercenary outfit like ACORN or SEIU. We are millions of Americans from across the political spectrum with minds of our own and ideas of our own. There is no national tea party teleprompter for us to read from.

This is just one guy's opinion. There are hundreds of even better ideas of where government spending can be cut - that's why we have comments at the end of this post. Since the President was kind enough to ask for our help, it is the least we can do to point him in the right direction. Let's hear 'em.

Tea Party Speech

(author's note: I speak to anyone who asks. In 2009 and 2010, I was invited to speak at a tea party rallies, and this is the transcript from one of them.)

I call it Tooth Fairy Government – that's where they take your quarter, put it under their kid's pillow and pretend they made the world 25 cents richer.

Now, the only people who believe in the Tooth Fairy are young children and old socialists. We should love our children and we should love our socialists, but we shouldn't let either of them run the country.

My name is Tim Nerenz, and I am a community organizer. I organize employees, customers, vendors, investors, and financiers to create prosperity for ourselves and for our families. I am an employer.

From our factories here in Wisconsin we compete around the world, and we compete against the world.

We can beat those nice folks who work in the factories of China, Mexico, Brazil, Viet Nam, Korea, Germany, Sweden, and Finland – we do it every day.

But we can't beat the folks who work in the cubicles in Washington and Madison.

From the minute she became Speaker of the House 3 ½ years ago, Nancy Pelosi declared war on Capitalism. President Obama is The Surge.

They promised to increase taxes, ration energy, nationalize key industries, unionize the rest, and establish a new minimum wage.

Mission accomplished. For 15 million Americans that new minimum wage is zero.

You can't be for jobs and against the businesses that create them.

Health Care. Cap and Trade. Card Check. And now the biggest tax increase in the history of the world.

Is that really what's wrong with this country? Our taxes are too low? We don't have enough regulations? Not enough laws? I don't think so.

Too much jockey, not enough horse – that is what's wrong with this country. That's *all* that's wrong with this country.

We need to quit whipping our private sector thoroughbred and start starving the 800 lb socialist jockey that is breaking our back.

You were not put on this earth to pull another man's plow. You were born to run free and proud, as fast and as far as your talent, effort, and faith will take you.

Throw off the yoke! Spit out the bit! Feel the wind in your face and reclaim your liberty this November.

This all started with Health Care last summer.

They had to take over health care because that's what they do in Europe, remember?

Now why on earth would we want to be like a place where they ban guns and sell speedos?

President Obama told us we would like government health care because they live longer in Europe.

Well, I don't know about you, but I don't care how old they are in Belgium, I would rather live free for 79 years than be a slave to the state for 81!

Thank you for coming out today to stand for liberty.

The Enemy of My Enemy

Libertarians are to conservatives what socialists are to liberals – ideological anchors that restrain drift to the unprincipled middle. Libertarian principles intensify the conservative message, and conservative political potency acquaints the public with libertarian themes. We need each other.

Just two short years ago, libertarian Ron Paul was ridiculed within his own Republican Party for demanding Constitutional limits on government, cutting government expenditures, calling for an audit of the Federal Reserve, opposing corporate bailouts, and warning against health care reform. He demonstrated the power of grass roots organizing and mobilizing new voters through internet social networking.

This is now the blueprint for success in GOP primaries; half of the candidates on the stump sound like Ron Paul this year and all of them have Facebook pages and e-mail lists. Rand Paul, Sharon Angle, Christie O'Connell, and Joe Miller all feature libertarian themes prominently in their anti-establishment campaigns. Glenn Beck, Vicki McKenna, Jonah Goldberg, Dennis Miller, Ann Coulter and George Will are just a few conservative opinion-shapers who acknowledge libertarian instincts.

The distinctly un-libertarian George W. Bush's presidency ultimately betrayed and alienated conservatives and libertarians alike, delivering control of government over to Pelosi and Obama. While we are distinct political philosophies, libertarians and conservatives share a common framework for understanding civil society, the role of the individual, and the role of government. We believe government is a necessary evil, something to be feared and caged and kept subservient to individual sovereignty.

Our libertarian/conservative worldview stands diametrically opposed to the socialist/liberal framework. Liberty versus Government – this is the great divide in American politics, not Party or demographic identity.

In electoral triage, divisions between libertarians and conservatives are cuts and bruises compared to the life-threatening wound that the socialist/liberal agenda is inflicting upon the nation. This year is not the time to let ideological purity deny a victory that our common interest has placed within reach; it is safe to ignore our differences long enough to defeat our common ideological adversary in November.

Which is not to say that we should rally behind all Republican candidates; libertarians and conservatives should rally behind candidates who share our commitment to liberty, be they Republicans, Libertarians, Constitution, independent, or by some miracle, Democrats.

The predicted Republican rout in November will occur not because of intelligent design from GOP Party leadership, but rather from the spontaneous order and organic energy of the tea party movement. That movement is not exclusively conservative; it includes many libertarian groups – Campaign 4 Liberty, Republican Liberty Caucus, Young Americans for Liberty, the 9/12 project, to name a few.

Some Libertarians are uncomfortable with the tea party; I am not one of them. For every one sign at a tea party advocating a position I disagree with, there are 20 which echo my sentiments. Overtly religious appeals do not offend me, patriotic symbols do not intimidate me, and alternative Constitutional interpretations do not obscure an underlying shared reverence for our founding principles.

Last weekend I was invited to speak at a tea party event in Merrillan, Wisconsin, population 587. The crowd was estimated at over 700; most of them, by show of hands, had never attended a political rally before. As I looked out over the audience, I recalled Grover Norquist's book title, "Leave Us Alone". That Merrillan crowd was the leave-us-alone coalition made flesh.

Whether their focus was education, taxes, debt, energy, guns, gold, religion, or any number of issues that matter most to them, most of those who gathered in Jackson County that day had a single non-negotiable demand of government, namely, to be left alone. And "leave us alone" is the essence of libertarian political philosophy – an uncompromising belief in the right of each individual to live free of coercive force.

The event's organizers knew I am a Libertarian. I wore my Libertarian Party lapel pin, signed some copies of my Libertarian book, and gave the same "Tooth Fairy Government" speech that I have given at Libertarian events. I was warmly received, as was Wisconsin libertarian icon Ed Thompson, who is running for state senate as a Republican. Those who view the tea party simply as a GOP subsidiary are badly mistaken.

This election year it is not difficult to determine friend and foe; what is difficult is trusting in the new coalition of Constitutionalists – including libertarians and conservatives - that has arisen in response to the clear and present danger that socialist/liberal statists pose to the nation.

The old saying goes, "the enemy of my enemy is my friend". Welcome, friends.

Or Else

Apparently I caused a bit of a stir this week when I suggested at a prestigious Milwaukee health care forum that the default setting for employers should be to opt out of health benefit coverage once public exchanges are up and running.

I honestly don't know what all the fuss is about. I merely said out loud what many, perhaps most, employers are thinking.

When Congress enacted the Affordable Care Act on March 23, employers were given a do-this-or-else ultimatum: provide the health insurance benefits specified by the federal government (do this) or pay fines and penalties (or else). They added 2,700 pages to confuse us, that's why this column is entitled "Moment of Clarity".

For the moment, let's just keep it that simple. Many, perhaps most, of us will choose "or else".

"Or else" is a perfectly rational choice, and the business decision, while emotionally difficult, is not particularly complicated. "Do this" has a cost of x and "or else" has a cost of y. Either x or y will be considerably less than the other depending on the circumstances of the firm once all the mandates, rules, regulations, fines, penalties, subsidies, vouchers, and reporting requirements are established.

Each employer will have a different circumstance based on the size, composition, and salary structure of their workforce; and each state will have its own public exchange rules, so the right answer will not be the same for everyone. The national statistical means and medians the experts used during the debate are useless – on average, human beings have one breast and one testicle, so what? Each firm and each family will act upon their own best interest. There are 27 million employers; no one can know how we will all decide three years from now.

But here is the default setting: the cost of opting out is a $2,000 fine per employee, while the cost of providing government-spec insurance will be around $12,000 per employee. That "or else"

---

advantage of $10,000 closes as the rest of the 2,700 pages of the Bill factor in, but the business case for "do this" is an uphill slog.

Within the next few months, all of us must begin to modify our plans to make them conform to the government's plan specification, which also limits our liability if we decide to drop. The President was not being truthful when he promised you the option of keeping your existing plan. That was never possible.

How could it be? Both sides in the health care debate have described the Affordable Care Act of 2010 the most significant change to our nation's health care system in 70 years. It is as if they made us play baseball for 7 decades, then changed the game to soccer and promised your employer would continue to bring the bats and gloves.

The law was passed; the game was changed. That was that; this is this.

So employers are putting on our shiny shorts and pulling up our white socks and running around kicking each other in the shins until that Mexican guy with three lungs starts screaming "GOAL". This, sadly, is the limit of my understanding of the most popular sport in the world, but I think you get the drift. 70 years of baseball is over; we are playing soccer now, so quit scratching yourself and dump the chew.

Now that we must all comply with a single template of coverage (or pay ridiculous fines for deviating), employers can't create a competitive advantage through benefit designs. Since that was their only purpose, the default setting is opt out, unless and until there is some new and compelling reason to offer benefits in lieu of cash.

In fact, opting out may just be the best strategy for recruiting top talent. If you are married to a school teacher, you probably prefer cash over insurance, since your family is already covered under your spouse's generous plan. As I said, the game has been changed.

Now, some have suggested it is immoral for employers to drop employee health insurance even if it is a good business decision. No, it is immoral to jack up fellow citizens with "do this or else" ultimatums. Not to mention it is unconstitutional, politically stupid, and arrogant beyond contempt. But the laws of economics and the law of unintended consequences do not yield to fiat and puffery and the impact of the Act is no longer in the hands of the politicians who passed it without reading.

Over the next three years, 27 million businesses are going to choose between "do this" and "or else". It will be a business decision based upon the incentives, not the intentions, of the Act. It will be made carefully, guided by the best interest of the firm and our employees, not by the ideological preferences of the Party temporarily in power in our nation's capital.

Americans who were promised by President Obama they could keep their current health insurance will discover it was not up to them, or him, to make that choice. That is his problem.

Market Failure

It still irks me to hear a politician or pundit describe the financial crisis of 2008 as a failure of capitalism, or the result of unregulated markets run amuck.

Let's remind ourselves what actually happened. The Fed-fueled housing bubble burst and sub-prime loans became toxic, causing the fractional reserve banking system to freeze and causing some major financial institutions to fail.

Stocks plummeted and the economy, already in recession, took a deep dive, despite trillions in government bailouts and stimulus programs. Unemployment skyrocketed as consumer spending and private investment were severely curtailed.

Where is the market failure in that?

The Fed is not a market creation. Fractional reserve banking is not a market creation. Sub-prime loans are not a market creation. Fannie and Freddie are government entities, AIG is a rigged monopoly, and each of the banks that received TARP bailout funds had regulators stationed right inside the bank's offices. The Community Reinvestment Act is not a market creation. Fiat money is not a market creation.

All of the components of the bubble, its collapse, and the failed bailout response were government interventions that prevented markets from functioning normally.

The 2008 meltdown and the subsequent two years of wrong-headed countermeasures prove nothing about capitalism or markets. What was proved was the error of Keynesian interventionist ideology. The meltdown and its aftermath show how woefully ignorant of basic economic principles our professional governing class has become.

Here is my challenge to the socialists who use the meltdown as a prop to rail against free markets: tell me specifically which element of capitalist economic theory "failed". Which law or axiom was disproved - was it marginal utility, price theory, substitution effect, division of labor, supply and demand, moral hazard, externalities, scarcity, the tragedy of the commons? Get out the econ text and point us to the chapter and page number.

Someone wisely said that blaming greed for the Wall St collapse is like blaming gravity for an airplane crash. Greed is a constant of the human condition. And like gravity needs to be countered by centrifugal force, markets need greed to be counterbalanced by the fear of losing everything.

Removing the fear of loss is like suspending centrifugal force – unchecked greed brings everything crashing violently to earth. That's the meltdown in a nutshell.

Did markets remove the fear of loss? No, it was government that did that through guarantees, bailouts, subsidies, Fed actions, and monetary policy that encouraged and rewarded bad behavior.

Markets punish bad behavior one transaction and one firm at a time, so we can learn from the mistakes of others. If one bank engages in risky lending and fails, thousands of other banks take note and act with prudence. Failure and bankruptcy transfer assets from poor stewards to good ones efficiently.

Government interventions, on the other hand, punish millions of innocents when they fail and we learn nothing from the obfuscations and outright lies of government actors covering their behinds and casting blame to anyone else but themselves.

To this day, you can not get Congressman Frank, Senator Dodd, Secretary Paulson, Chairman Greenspan, or any of the central figures in this tragedy to admit to a single thing they themselves did wrong over the past decade. They talk of "systemic risk" as if it were a bacterial infection, rather than the consequences of their own decisions and actions.

It is only central bank monetary policy and interventionist fiscal policy that creates the boom and bust cycles in the economy. It is why the founding fathers did not authorize a central bank in the Constitution. They understood that sound money, free trade, and low taxes were the keys to prosperity. In the hundred years since we created the central bank and went to fiat money, we have proven the Founders to be right over and over again.

You probably know a banker. Can you imagine a bunch of real bankers having coffee and thinking up ways to grow their banks when one says "hey, I got a great idea, boys – let's loan money to people who can't pay it back!"

Do you think they would lend unlimited amounts of their own bank's money to people with no job and no income at 4% interest? Of course not; the subprime racket could only exist if there was a sucker – i.e. the federal government – to buy the loan and guarantee against the loss.

There is failure in markets all the time; those suppliers least able to compete fail. Failure is an essential component of free enterprise; it makes room for new entrants, new products and services, and new ways of conducting exchange.

The market system did not fail in 2008; the government's attempts to manage it did.

Negative Ads

One of the side benefits of international business travel is that it has mercifully taken me out of Wisconsin during this election home stretch when every other television advertisement is a slanderous attack against a political opponent.

If you really, truly think that Scott Walker's goal as Governor is to take health care away from children, or that Tom Barrett's first priority would be to dump Milwaukee's raw sewage into the rest of the state's waterways, then you should just sit this one out and hold on tight to that one marble you have left.

There are plenty of perfectly good reasons to vote for or against either Mr. Walker or Mr. Barrett, and for that matter, all of the candidates from all of the parties in all of the races all over Wisconsin this year. It's not like we don't know what's at stake already, or don't know the candidates and their positions.

When a candidate promises more government and less liberty, he has already run the most effective negative ad against himself. When she disregards the Constitution, disrespects opposition, panders and preens and sells out to campaign donors' provincial interests, the elevator has already reached the basement.

When we see Satan's horns and tail in plain view, do we care if he double-claimed an energy tax credit for weatherproofing the gates of hell? The dude is already Satan; quit piling on before I start to feel sorry the guy.

Attack ads are like porn – designed to titillate, not educate. There must be a handful of studios that crank these suckers out like an assembly line. Queue up the scary music, close in on the regular-folk actors sitting around a table who turn to worry into the camera, then quote some headlines with newsprint graphics in background, and roll to the big finish: "Call Demi Democrat and tell her to stop eating children."

Paid for by Citizens Against Every Bad Thing. Yawn. And both establishment parties run these ads; I believe it is one of the principle reasons so many people have abandoned them to join third parties or vote as independents.

Political operatives will tell you that attack ads are effective, but that is like asking a priest his opinion of confession. The pols make their living marketing candidates and their idea of winning is coming in second in an ugly contest. This election is all about dumping the status quo, and status quo political advertising should be on the hit list.

We already have low expectations, and still they find new ways to disappoint. When Jerry Brown's campaign called Meg Whitman a whore, the only thing missing was the perfunctory, "and I approved this message." I gave him the benefit of the doubt until I saw his apology – my son used to fake it better than that to try to avoid the timeout.

Personally, I find it all degrading, this televised orgy of bottom feeding. Give me a candidate who can tell me what is wrong and what he/she would do to fix it. Tell me what his principles are so I can compare them to mine. Convince me that she deserves to represent me, that she would be a worthy tenant of my trust. Show me that he understands and respects the Constitution. Opponent is wrong – ok; opponent is evil – over the line.

Note to candidates: this is a job interview and we are the boss. Would you dump a load of garbage into my office hoping to win the job? Then don't do it in my home every night.

White Dudes

A recent commentary on the tea party movement described it as "a bunch of white dudes afraid of losing their monopoly on power." Maybe somewhere, but not down on this planet; our white dude monopoly was busted several decades ago.

For those who may not have noticed, our President is black, his first Chief of Staff was Jewish, and the Speaker of the House is female. Our Secretary of State is female; she succeeded a black female, whose predecessor was black. The Chairman of the House Ways and Means Committee is black, the Chairman of the Banking Committee is gay, and the first head of the President's Council of Economic Advisors is female.

Please tell me, where is the great white dude monopoly?

In our largest state, the Governor of California is an immigrant; a female ex-CEO is running to succeed him, while another female ex-CEO is running to unseat one of the two incumbent female Senators. The GOP has a black chairman and a female presidential frontrunner, or Pete's sake. The Tea Party has delivered primary victories to Hispanic, black, and female candidates at the expense of their white male counterparts. There isn't a single WASP on the Supreme Court.

Call me old-fashioned, but I like my white dude monopolies to have a few more white dudes in them. Makes the story better.

As it turns out, government incompetence is an equal opportunity employer. For all the hoopla about the benefits of diversity in theory, it has proven to be a big-so-what in the real world. The government of not-white-dudes is no better than the government of white dudes was. This comes as no surprise to us white dudes.

President Obama has hinted that opposition to his policies is really about white dudes being uncomfortable with a black President. Wrong. We are uncomfortable with *this* black President – not because he is black, but because he sucks at being President.

If you gave Ron Paul a mocha dip, the Liberty movement would not notice. And if you blanched Mr. Obama and gave him red hair and freckles, the signs would still say "Hands Off My Health Care" at the Tea Party rallies across the nation.

Race and gender are assigned to us in the womb – they are not achievements we should expect to be either rewarded or punished for. The measure of a person is what we have made of ourselves in this world, not the characteristics nature issued to us at arrival.

Each individual is a fully formed child of God, endowed with free will and capable of nobility and depravity, courage and cowardice, avarice and charity. Some of us are white dudes, and more of us are not.

Big deal.

Thank You, Nancy

For the next week, partisan forecasters will spar over the precise number of seats that will change hands in the midterms, but a few races here or there will not obscure the plain meaning of this election: it's one and done for the Pelosi/Obama socialist agenda.

In one sense, we owe them both a debt of gratitude, for it was their legislative overreaching and transparent disdain for ordinary Americans that ignited the liberty movement and fueled the passion of the tea parties.

Creeping socialism is difficult to see plainly; it took comrade Nancy's because-I-deemed-it-mister style to awaken the American public to the threat.

It was her blithe dismissal of the Constitution ("are you serious?") that united the libertarians, conservatives, constitutionalists, and free-thinking independents in renewed opposition to the unchecked expansion of government power.

"We have to pass the bill to find out what is in the bill" has moved ahead of "Let them eat cake!" as the #1 all-time fury-inciting utterance in the clueless female category. It makes anything Christine O'Donnell ever said seem positively Socratic.

This midterm election has become more than a referendum on President Obama; it has become a referendum on government itself. Every major race across the nation can be reduced to this essential question: do we want more government or less? In the third year of a recession with no end in sight, and the ninth year in a foreign war without a clear victory strategy, few Americans have any appetite for more.

The impotence of the BP spill response and the incompetence of the economic stimulus response clearly measured the distance between the swell government that is promised and the pathetic one that is practiced. Only the most rigid liberal ideologue still believes in tooth fairy government in the fourth year of Speaker Pelosi's disastrous reign.

We have seen enough. On November 2, the American people will not simply choose candidate A over candidate B; we will choose liberty over government, capitalism over socialism, the private sector over the public, the liberty movement over the arrogance of party establishments.

The only question to be decided in this last week of the campaign is the magnitude of the rout - will it be a tidal wave, an avalanche, or a tsunami? And who cares? The point will be made, and the sprint towards socialism will be stopped in its tracks, and the first step in reclaiming our liberty will be taken.

And for the first time in four years, we will have a reason to say, "Thank You, Nancy".

Self-inflicted

No, my dear Democrat friends, it wasn't secret money from overseas, or the media failure to explain health care, or talk radio hosts, or Fox News, or the racist tea parties, or Americans for Prosperity that cost you the election today – you did this to yourselves.

It started with the TARP bank bailouts; the American people were 8:1 opposed and you passed it anyway – twice. Then the stimulus; overwhelmingly opposed but you passed that, too. Then you hosed the bond-holders and gave GM and Chrysler to the unions – they took our $50 billion and went bankrupt anyway. Don't forget foreclosure relief that let people default twice on our nickel – it was the bankruptcy attorneys that loved you for that one, not us.

And then there was health care; you had three chances to bail out with dignity but you rammed it down our throats instead. You threatened to "deem it" if you couldn't get the votes, even though two thirds of the American people were against your bill – a bill so ridiculous you had to pass it to learn what was in it. Just to rub it in, you nationalized student loans in an 11th hour amendment.

Next came the BP oil spill; three months of looking around for an ass to kick but having no trouble finding the right one to kiss – preventing foreign assistance to please your union masters again. And then there was the bailout of the teachers' unions – overriding every single school board and state department of education in the nation who had not seen fit to raise compensation in a fiscal crisis.

Should I go on? Cap and Trade, Cash-4-Clunkers, the President's 60 rounds of golf, Michelle's Spanish vacation, your two any-gal-will-do Supreme Court appointments, tanking the Fed audit, suing Arizona, ACORN's hidden camera fiasco, letting the Black Panthers walk, re-appointing Ben Bernanke, and the internet kill switch.

You adjourned your session, allowing the largest tax increase in the history of the world to take effect without the courtesy of a vote. You failed to adjust the AMT in your haste to hit the campaign trail. You offered a $250 check to seniors after you gutted their Medicare and hit them with a 55% inheritance tax – as if you could bribe the Greatest Generation anyway.

Your economic plan was worse than nothing. 15 million Americans are out of work, 9 million more are underemployed, and another 1.2 million have quit looking altogether. Home values are falling, the dollar is falling, real GDP is falling; the only thing going up is gold, unless you count the national debt and the number of troops you keep sending to a war you don't know how to win.

You called us racist. You called us dumb. You called us enemies, hicks, astro-turf, the great unwashed. You made fun of our reverence for the Constitution and our commitment to our faiths. You don't like our guns, our trucks, our groceries, our hobbies, our rallies, our Facebook Pages, or our women who think for themselves - witches, bitches, and whores, you called them. You hate it when we prosper, and you hate *us* when we speak our minds.

How could you possibly expect that we would vote for you after all that? No, seriously – did you really think we would reward you at the polls? Did you?

Your wounds are all self-inflicted. You turned the Democratic Party of JFK into the Social Democrat Party of Dean, Pelosi, Obama, Frank, Krugman, and ACORN. You turned government into an ultimatum and we picked "or else". You tried to make America into France, so we said, "au revoir". You thought your ends justified your means, so we introduced you to *our* ends.

That's what happened today - it wasn't done *to* you by anyone else, you did it to yourselves.

The coalition of conservatives, libertarians, constitutionalists, and independents that purged unprincipled Republicans in the primaries and cleansed the Congress today will not go lay by our dish just because Nancy Pelosi has been dethroned. Our mission did not end yesterday, it has only begun.

CAPITALISTA!

So my advice to all of the new Republican members of the next Congress is this: don't sign a *three* year lease on that townhouse in Georgetown. Do what we sent you to do and you will be re-elected; if not, then you will be tossed onto the gut-pile of phonies who say one thing to get our vote and then do another once they are in Washington.

You guys work for us, not the other way around. We fired the Republicans in 2006; they brought it on themselves. And we fired the Democrats today; they brought it on themselves. Here's a tip: if you want to avoid being on the receiving end in 2012, try being a little nicer to the boss.

You have four jobs to do: revive the economy, revive the economy, revive the economy, and revive the economy.

You have just seen four years of what *not* to do from Nancy Pelosi, George W. Bush, Ben Bernanke, and President Obama. If they passed it, repeal it; if they raised it, cut it; if they banned it, liberate it; if they were for it, don't do it; if they were against it, then let 'er rip.

Yes, it is that easy. We did our part, now go do yours.

Au Revoir

No election cycle would be complete without some Hollywood liberal threatening to move to France because the Democrats lost. This year it was some B-lister I never heard of, but my reflexive response is the same as it was for Sean Penn, Alec Baldwin, or that Janine person – au revoir, mon ami.

Seriously, despondent liberals should not just talk about moving to France, they should move to France. Nothing is stopping them, and if they can't get a visa to say there, just camp out illegally – what's good for the goose and all that. And if the French try to deport them, then Attorney General Holder can sue and we can all boycott French goods - given that they don't make anything in France, that will be painless and impotent symbolism, so we can all know what if feels like to be a liberal.

Our ancestors all left one country where the government was intolerable and moved to another where they could achieve their dreams. Back then it was a lot tougher to pull off – no money, cholera, and they could not text their BFF's in the old country to tell them how OMG awesome their new life is and how much they heart it here LOL plus that winky parenthesis thing. Moving to France now is a piece of cake.

Our fore-parents' idea of a civil society was freedom and individual responsibility, and they came here because that is what we had to offer. They left Paris to settle North Dakota – that's how much they loved freedom. Most arrived poor and become rich. Liberals today would be going to France richer and would become poorer, but that is their idea of the winning formula, so the only thing holding them back is the lack of a government bailout Bill that would pay for the move.

Liberals miserable in the United States would love France, and not just for the mistresses and red berets. They have high taxes, unions, carbon limits, socialized medicine, early retirements, long lunches, generous pensions, bicycles and trains, backpacks, permanent unemployment, and lots and lots of time off. Seriously, if that is your idea of a civil society, then go over there and live large. Why knock yourselves out trying to bring all of that stuff over here, when you can simply move yourself over there? Go! Vamos! Oops, wrong country.

Most Americans don't expect everyone else to change to accommodate our desires; we change our own circumstances when something is deemed intolerable. People who don't like the weather in Maine move to California. People who don't like being unemployed in Massachusetts move to North Carolina. People bullied in a small town for being different move to the city. People leave the crime of the city to move to the suburbs. People overtaxed in Wisconsin move to Florida. If limited government is simply more than you can bear, then move to France – or Venezuela, or Cuba, or Myanmar or someplace where there it is not limited. Be happy.

Here's where liberals get confused: the United States of America and its federal government are *not the same thing*. The latter is the hired hand of the former, tasked with providing a few basic services that benefit all Americans equally – single currency, national defense, transportation infrastructure, a court system to protect rights and property – within the constraints of the Constitution and the amount of the taxes we give it to spend.

This nation is its people, not its government. For nearly a century we have drifted farther and farther away from this essential truth of our system of self-government. There is nothing wrong with this nation; the problem is our government.

The nation hires its government for $2.4 trillion in taxes; the government spends an additional $1.4 trillion that is steals from our grandchildren.

The nation last declared war in 1941; the government has initiated eight foreign conflicts on its own since then.

The nation provides for those in need generously through private charity; the government perpetuates poverty and dependence on state-run welfare programs.

The nation creates jobs, starts new businesses, and stimulates innovation; the government stifles economic growth and regulates mediocrity.

The nation makes its citizens unequally richer; the government makes us equally poorer.

Liberals expect too much from government. When Americans reflect on the richness of our lives, we remember family, friends, co-workers, team-mates, neighbors, teachers, pastors, mentors, students, congregation members, customers, employees, bosses, fellow volunteers in charities, club-mates, our favorite sports teams, authors, singers, actors, and writers – we do not recall assistant deputy undersecretaries of the Department of Interior.

I can still name all of the starters for the Green Bay Packers of the 1960's, but I couldn't tell you who the Governor of Wisconsin was in any one of their championship years, or why it was that we just hadta-hadta-hadta vote for him and not the other dude. And that is exactly as it should be. Somebody ran the state for a while – must have done ok at it, because we are not part of Minnesota.

Government should barely matter. We have each other for the important stuff; we just need someone to plow the interstate so we can do things together. Liberals, conservatives, and libertarians get along just fine until it comes to government and politics. Our common goal should be to limit that interruption in our otherwise happy relationship, to make it as infrequent and unimportant as humanly possible.

No one should have to move to France if Republicans win an election, or move to Singapore if the Democrats do. I don't know where all the hard-cores would go if we Libertarians ever won an election, but the folks coming here from all over the world to live free would be an upgrade over the mud-sticks moving out, I can promise you that.

Les goûts et les couleurs ne se dicutent pas. Au Revoir!

PART TWO: LAME DUCK SESSION

November 2010 – January 2011

It's Still Your Money

Every so often, I feel compelled to remind my readers that the only moral transaction between equally self-sovereign persons is voluntary exchange.

Either you believe that you alone own your person and the fruits of your labor, or you believe someone else has a superior claim.

At one end of the political spectrum, socialists believe that "society" has a superior claim to your person; at the far other end, libertarians believe that your claim to personhood is absolute. Liberals and conservatives fall in between the extremes.

When liberals and conservatives debate tax policy, their arguments rage over the amount and proportion of individual income that should be justly confiscated by the State. The principled libertarian does not take the bait - confiscation is immoral, regardless and the correct answer is zero.

Warren Buffet recently supported increasing taxes on wealthy Americans, asking, "Who should pay more - the waitress that brings my coffee or me?"

Here is a more interesting question: why does the principle of "each according to his ability" apply only to taxes and not to the price of the coffee that the waitress serves.

Mr. Buffet is free to pay whatever amount he feels is appropriate for the cup of coffee the waitress delivers to him. Just like Mr. Buffet is free to pay whatever amount of taxes he feels is his duty.

There is no moral argument that compels him to wait until we all join him in his personal opinion of what is fair.

Few, if any, wealthy liberals volunteer to pay the higher tax rates that they advocate for everyone. This defeats the moral argument for increased taxation.

Would you continue to rape, or murder, or assault until everyone else stops? Then why continue to pay less tax, if you sincerely believe you are doing harm?

The top marginal tax rate for individuals is 35%; President Obama wants to raise that to 39%. Mr. Buffet, one of the richest Americans has said that he pays 17%.

When you get that up that up to 35%, sir, then I will listen to your argument for why the rest of us should pay 39%. Not before.

Difficult, Not Complicated

When it comes to government spending, railing against it while running for office is a heck of a lot easier than doing it once you are elected – we all get that. But while the task of carving the federal budget to size is difficult, it is not complicated.

In a previous post, I listed the dozens of agencies and departments that would be eliminated if we libertarians ran the government. We would cut taxes, cut spending, and run a surplus that paid down the debt. For some, that was a bit too radical, so this week I'll tone it down a little to propose something a more modest.

The size of the hole in the budget is $1.3 trillion; the government takes $2.4 trillion in taxes and spends $3.7 trillion. Our government's debt is $13.8 trillion and rising at $4 billion per day. These are mind-numbing sums.

Just drop off the last 8 zeros and everyone can get their head around our budget problem. Imagine you make $24,000 and spend $37,000; you have run up run up $138,000 on our Visa card and they won't increase your credit limit. Your boss (the taxpayers) won't give you a raise (tax increase), so what do you do? Cut your spending by $14,000 and sell things you can live without.

We have all been there at some point in our lives. It's not complicated; it's just difficult.

A spending cut of $1.3 trillion is 35%; and when we say it that way, it sounds impossible. In fact, we should quit talking about "cuts" and talk about how much government we need and how much we can afford. So instead of saying a 35% cut, lets say rolling the price of government back to what it was in 2006.

That's right – all of the screaming and wailing and gnashing of teeth about to come raining down on us from Washington D.C. in the coming months is about spending the same amount on government as we did the first year Brett Favre retired. That's what it would take to balance the budget. Not 1906, just to 2006.

In 2006, $2.4 trillion was enough to run the government, clean up after Katrina, and fight two wars overseas. One of those wars is over, and the Katrina clean-up is well-behind us, so why is it so hard to imagine that we might be able to operate the machinery of a civilized nation on $2.4 trillion a year?

There is no practical way to change entitlement programs this year, and we will spend $1.4 trillion on them. That leaves us $1 trillion to do everything else. Any government-type worth their salt would say "no way" to that. Way.

Do you remember the year 2000? Were anarchy, cannibalism, and lawless gang rule the order of the day? Democrats recall it fondly as the golden era of good government – the happy time before George W. Bush broke the world.

They should recall that their most wonderful year of wonderful government wonderfulness - before Bush plunged us into the dark ages - was operated at an *inflation-adjusted* cost of $1.2 trillion in 2010 dollars. Were the guys in the cubes so much smarter then that only they could pull off this miracle? I think not. In fact, it's probably the same guys in the same cubes.

Now, if you blame Obama for this mess, then you must support the rollback to government spending at 2006 levels, before he came to Washington and ruined everything. If you blame Bush, then you must support spending at the inflation adjusted levels that you had before *he* came to Washington. See – bipartisanship is not complicated, either; just a quibble over the date to which we should rollback government..

Defending our nation cost an inflation-adjusted $376 billion in 2000. That was sufficient to establish unquestioned global military superiority then and it is now. Had we spent $2 trillion or $20 trillion, it would not have prevented 9/11; we cannot maintain a state of perpetual war, and the regimes we aimed to destroy have been destroyed. We should not only stand down our dozens of permanent garrisons around the world, but sell the properties – raising revenue and easing our deficit problem.

But now comes the difficult part. To roll back government to where it was in 2000, we will have to eliminate all the featherbed jobs added the bureaucracy since then and roll back federal employee pay scales to the rate of inflation. Federal compensation has outpaced inflation by 33% over the last decade and this "windfall" – won't they love that term – has lifted average federal compensation to $129,000, about twice the average in the private sector.

So isn't this fun: the people who scream the loudest about preserving Medicare and Social Security get to do something about it – give back their own windfall increases. Or they could throw in with greedy CEO's and wall street bonus babies and demand to hang on to their ill-gotten gains, forcing all the blue-heads to eat dog food and live in dumpsters.

If you have been keeping score, we are only $200 billion away from balancing the budget *this year* without raising taxes or cutting entitlements. $100 billion of that goes away thanks to the FED's insanely low interest rates and their beneficial effect on interest payments against our national debt. Open up oil and gas leasing and sell off some land and we can raise $100 billion easy.

There you go – budget balanced and no need to lift the debt ceiling, default on our debt, raise taxes, or destroy our currency.

Waterboy

As the debate over extending the Bush tax cuts starts up again, liberals continue to call no change a "cut", and call a cut "spending". Which brings us to the most significant question in matters of fiscal policy: what is wrong with these people?

Honestly - they have diplomas from very expensive colleges and prep schools; they read a lot and have dinners with people who are really smart, and yet they can not comprehend terms whose meaning is plain to any 7th grader – spend, earn, tax, own.

Reasonable people can have good faith disagreements over matters of policy, but misleading the public by torturing the vocabulary is not acting in good faith, it is deceitful, disrespectful, and disgraceful.

David Axelrod argued the lie again today when he said we can't afford to spend our money on a tax cut for the rich when there are more important things to spend it on.   Where to begin....a) leaving rates alone is not a *cut*, b) keeping your money is not *spending*, and c) it is not *our* money, it belongs to whoever earned it. But these are the liberal talking points, repeated over and over and over again, as if the quantity of repetition might improve the quality of the argument. It won't.

The no-tax-increase-is-spending argument is absurd on its face. If not raising taxes is the same as spending, then is electing not to steal money from a church the same as making a contribution? Do you think the IRS will let me deduct all the money I was going to steal from charities but then decided to let them keep?

And speaking of church, may I remind all you tax-the-rich liberals that the Ten Commandments admonish against stealing, testifying falsely, and *coveting*. As Hannibal Lector explained to Special Agent Starling, the first pathology of the cannibal is what?   He covets.   Coveting is also the first pathology of redistributive economic theory.

The liberal notion that all money is "our money" is ridiculous and historically curious. Was it not the feminist movement that brought us separate checkbooks? If the money that you earn cannot even be shared with your own spouse, then how in heck do you talk yourself into a joint account with all 310 million other Americans? I guess if you spend all of your energy feeling, your thinking skills atrophy.

Borrowing an analogy from economist Arthur Laffer, here is Keynesian economics for dummies: the liberals think you raise the water level of the pool by taking a bucketful from the deep end and pouring it into the shallow end. When it doesn't work, their answer is more buckets – more and more and more and more buckets. This sounds like a terrific idea if you make your living hauling water.

But the rest of us understand that the more water there is in the buckets, the less there is in the pool. That is what is wrong with our economy, and it won't get any better until this government stops borrowing money to hire more waterboys. Cutting taxes – actually cutting them – empties the water out of the government buckets into the private sector pool, raising the tide and lifting the boats.

The people in the shallow end of the pool need to learn how to swim over to the better life in the deep end on their own. Pouring water on their head doesn't help them; it only makes the waterboys feel useful. And it is bankrupting the nation.

Here is an easy way to put and end to this whole tax-the-rich nonsense: we simply drop the threshold for "rich" down from $250,000 to $129,500 – the average compensation of federal employees. That will allow federal workers, all the union bosses and Congressmen to help spread the wealth around. Still think it is good idea, lefties? I didn't think so.

We will pay $2.4 trillion in taxes this year. That is enough. That was enough to run the whole government in 2006, including funding two wars and the post-Katrina cleanup. Is it so difficult to imagine that we could operate a civil government for that sum now that one of those wars is over and Katrina is four more years behind us?

When the Statists start screaming and wailing and gnashing their teeth over "draconian" spending cuts needed to balance the budget, just think about your life in 2006. The Dow was headed toward 14,000 and unemployment was under 5%. Your home was worth more, your 401(k) was worth more, and the dollar was worth more. Was it so awful?

It's not *our* money; it's *your* money. You keeping what you have earned is not a tax cut, and it is not government spending. Anyone who says otherwise is a fool, a liar or a waterboy; and we should not let fools, liars, and waterboys run the country.

American Pie

Here is the difference: socialists fret over giving everyone an equal slice of the pie, while capitalists bake more pies. Which is better - abundance distributed unequally, or an equal ration of scarcity? Capitalists choose abundance.

Wealth is created when materials, labor, and capital are employed to add value. The baker takes $1 worth of ingredients (material) mixes and kneads and rolls and forms it (labor) and bakes in an oven (capital), and creates a pie worth $6 to the market – i.e. you, the consumer. The pie is wealth; the $5 of value-added realized in the exchange is the measure of it.

The illusion of wealth is not wealth; the dollars exchanged for the pie are not pie. True prosperity is measured in pies, and economic growth is the making of more pie, not the printing of more money. If Ben Bernanke devalues the inch by 50%, it doesn't make me grow, even though the FED's tape will "prove" that I am 12 feet tall.

Everyday, our nation of bakers goes to work and makes pies – that is real GDP. Is there any more pie when the Federal Reserve adds $600 billion of "quantitative easing"? Is there more pie when Congress extends unemployment benefits? Is there more pie when government increases the baker's taxes? Is there more pie if the EPA rations energy to the baker for his ovens? Is there more pie if the oven must be made in the USA? Is there more pie if the baker is forced to pay his helpers higher wages? Is there more pie if they are forced to join a union? No, no, no, no, no, no and no.

Is there more pie when we force the baker to provide health care or pay a fine? Is there more pie when the Department of Pies mandates standardized national pie testing? Is there more pie when government employees of DOP get a pay raise? Is there more pie when we invade another country? Is there more pie if we borrow money from the Chinese to pay interest on the debt we owe to the Saudis? Or use it to bail out a few big banks' gambling losses? Or subsidize unprofitable corporations? Or give pay raises to teachers? No, no, no, no, no, no, no, no and no.

And they wonder why the economy is not growing. How could we expect a group of anti-capitalist lawyers, politicians, and academics with virtually no business experience to craft a pro-growth economic policy that would encourage businesses to form, grow, and prosper? It would have been sensible to ask the bakers how we could make more pies; instead they called us names and blamed us for their mistakes.

The socialists have had their turn; we have gone hungry for three years now since their baker's rack of cards collapsed in an embarrassing Epic Fail. They have no idea how to fix it, because they have no clue that they broke it in the first place. It is time for them to step aside and let the capitalists do what we do best – make more pies.

Step one is to lower taxes on work, savings, capital, profit, and trade. There *is* no other way to stimulate economic growth. To make more pies, we need more bakers willing to add more ovens, and use more energy, streamline processes, invent new methods, hire more workers and insure they employed more productively. Bakers will not risk their life savings and work day and night to enrich the IRS.

Step two is to deregulate markets, liberate the workplace, and end subsidies so choice and competition can flourish. There *is* no other way to unlock the potential of our best and brightest entrepreneurs, workers, and traders. The only way workers will ever make more money in the bakery is if they bake more pies. And innovation only happens through competition, and competition only happens in free markets, and by that I mean free from government control and mandatory unionization.

Step three is to celebrate our most successful capitalists, not demonize them. Their desire for more profit is what drives down costs, and lower costs drive down prices. And the more that capitalists drive down prices, the more pies people can buy for themselves and their families. Not just more affordable pies, but a greater variety of pies – lots and lots of different kinds of delicious pies.

Capitalism brings about an abundance of pie. There *is* no other way to produce surplus; abundance is freedom's greatest gift.

Capitalism is waiting to give it to us, but we are denying it to ourselves.

Because the socialists hate free-range pie. They want to control it and allocate it, and direct it to their own purposes. Their beloved government can not create pie; it can only redistribute; taking the pies from the people who made them and giving them to people who did not, and eating half along the way. Socialists call this *justice*; that is their opinion. But they also call it *prosperity*; and that is demonstrably wrong.

If you have two pies, you are wealthier than when you have one, are you not? If I bake ten pies, are you any less wealthy? No, you are not. If the State taxes away our surplus pies we both have one pie – equality has been achieved. But are you wealthier with your one equality pie than when you had two and I had ten? No, you are not. You are poorer. That's what socialism delivers in the name of equality. Always. Everywhere. Every time.

So we are both less wealthy - and we are angry. We blame each other for our anger; we both think the other is greedy, and we both fear we will starve to death as a result. What was taken from us was more valuable than the pie; it was the good will and peace that once existed between us. Capitalists did not divide us; the socialists did that.

On some other planet, where wise angels rule over nations of saints, I would be a socialist, too; but we live on this one, and we have 5,000 years of communal mistakes to learn from. Free market capitalism is the only economic system compatible with the ideal of individual liberty; voluntary exchange is the only moral transaction between equal sovereigns.

We need more pie, not smaller equal slices.

Saving Social Security

For more than 50 years, Democrats and Republicans have known that us baby boomers were going to bankrupt the Social Security system; and for more than 50 years they have both kicked the can down the road. Welcome to the end of the road.

Only the seriously delusional still pretend that any real funds have been accumulated in the Social Security Trust Fund. You can't spend the same dollar twice, and we have raided the fund year after year to pay for other current government services. What is in the "Lock Box" are some worthless junk bonds issued by a government that is trillions in debt and a few months away from default - the deadbeat government in question is the United States of America. That is so painful to say out loud.

Every time a panel is formed to look at Social Security reform, the answer comes back the same: extend the age of eligibility, increase the payroll tax, and reduce the benefits paid. And Congress does none of them. Reduce the benefit and the blue-heads won't vote for you; raise the tax and working people won't vote for you; extend the age of eligibility and nobody will vote for you. It is impossible for politicians to do what needs to be done – coercion is hard work.

That's why we Libertarians prefer to do things the easy way – ask for volunteers, and leave the politicians and bureaucrats out of it. Most people will gladly pitch in to save Social Security; you just need to ask them *nicely*.

Lately, I have been asking this question when I speak to groups with lots of baby boomers in the crowd: how many of you would continue working past the age of 65 if you didn't have to pay *any* taxes on what you earned? Almost all the hands go up; there you go - problem solved. I call it Pension Choice.

The idea is ridiculously simple: at age 65, you retire....from paying taxes on earned income. That's right - zero, zilch, nada. You will not pay any income tax, payroll tax, capital gains tax, or tax on dividends if you decide to keep working full time and defer the draw on your social security benefits. Look at the gross earnings on your pay stub – you get *that* number in the bank. Sweet.

You have suffered enough; you have carried the world on your shoulders for five decades and it is time to lay your burden down. We thank you for your service; enjoy the full fruits of your remaining labors. You decide - if you want to retire at 65 and draw benefits under the current system, go ahead; if you want to keep working and keep everything you make, go ahead.

No one is adversely impacted by the decision of any another person, and no one is coerced into doing something they do not want to do – the founders called that novel concept the "pursuit of happiness", and we should put it to use more often.

Every day past 65 that you work is one less day the government has to pay you benefits, and one less day that someone else who is working has to pay for those benefits. Win-win. Medicare and all the other unfunded pension plans (which are about to default) would be de-stressed and salvaged as well when individuals elect to defer their retirement age. Win, win, win. Everybody wins, but not everyone will be happy.

Socialists and statists will whine and pout and pitch a fit because they don't get to tell you what to do; let 'em all cry in their living-wage, eco-bean mocha latte. We should have told them to stick it years ago, before they morphed Uncle Sam into creepy Uncle Ernie with one hand in our pockets and the other down our pants.

But what about all the lost tax revenues from the people who keep working? What tax revenues – they were going to retire, remember? We weren't going to collect any taxes anyway, so the loss of revenues to the IRS is negligible, while the savings in deferred benefits is substantial. If only one person defers it is a good thing; if several million do, it is a really good thing. Even the economists at CBO could get this one right – maybe.

And besides, it is the value you add with your labor that creates prosperity and economic growth, not the taxes the government rakes off the top. Having millions more productive, value-adding citizens engaged in bona fide economic activity is what will propel this nation out of its coma; not quantitative easing, or faux stimulus spending, or accounting gimmickry, or redistributive economic folly.

Introducing Pension Choice does not make the Social Security system a good deal; there is nothing that can do that. Over time, it must be converted from a promise of defined public benefits to a personal asset funded with defined contributions – I think we all know that. But to do so responsibly will take a generation, and we need to save Social Security right now so people who have paid in for 50 years have something to show for it – either tax abatement or pension draw as each sees fit.

The right-here-and-now problem of extending eligibility dates and reducing benefits is easily solved without confiscation and coercion, as difficult as that notion is for statists to comprehend. And now that there are no earmarks allowed, the Pension Choice law could be written on one page and voted in a day.

So why not; does anyone in Congress – from either party - have a better idea? Let's hear it.

Shanghai

Recently I made my first visit to China, and two statues in Shanghai's famous Bund district spoke volumes of that country's amazing transformation: along the river stands a bronze of Chairman Mao, while the entrance to East Nanjing Road is guarded by the bronze of a woman shopping.

There was no one getting their picture taken with Chairman Mao; but the line to pose with the shopping lady bent around the corner. That is my lasting memory of Shanghai.

To hell with the bowl haircuts and unisex grey uniforms; the women of China have discovered make-up, iPods, leather jackets, and shoes. And the men of China have discovered women, now that you can tell them from the boys.

I asked the hostess in my hotel's business center what freedom means to her. Her answer was, "more". Asked more of what, her answer was, "everything".

That pretty well sums up the economic policy of the country. If you walk, you want a bicycle; if you have a bicycle you want a moped; if you have a moped, you want a scooter; if you have a scooter you want a car; if you have car, you want a big car; if you have a big car, you want a driver.

Nanjing Road is an upscale pedestrian shopping way in the heart of Shanghai; the Time's Square of China's largest city and its center of commerce. At 11:00 pm, the neon lights go dim, the crowds disperse, and the music stops.

When I asked the concierge why there is a curfew, he was puzzled by the question, then responded, "No curfew; everyone in bed - must work in the morning."

And that, my friends, is why the Chinese are kicking our butts.

Welfare To Work

Commenting on last week's post, Pension Choice, a reader questioned how we would provide jobs for younger workers if older workers postponed their retirements. Once again, my libertarian solution for jobs is ridiculously simple: eliminate the corporate income tax.

Before you let fly with the angry anti-corporate letters, bear in mind the corporate income tax only brings in about $300 billion in a good year, while estimates of the costs of corporate subsidies, bailouts, price supports, and the like run as high as $350 billion. There are now over 1,800 subsidy programs, a number that has doubled in the past 20 years.

Eliminating both the corporate income tax and all corporate subsidies provides instant deficit relief as well as triggering an economic boom that will make China look like Sheboygan Junior Achievement. So let's do welfare-to-work for the Fortune 500 and let the other 2.7 million American corporations compete on a level playing field for once.

Now, you won't hear this proposal coming out of Washington, because the statists in both establishment parties love tax subsidies like Lindsay Lohan loves snorting coke in a stolen fur. Subsidies are what generates the return on investment in lobbying and campaign contributions; tax breaks and earmarked spending are the only things that politicians have to offer fat-cat donors in exchange for their millions.

Eliminate the selective corporate tax credits and subsidies and we liberate the legislative process from the corrupting grip of special interest money. Eliminate the corporate income tax entirely and we insure that all the zombies remain in their graves. And the static-score deficit reduction of $50 billion is mice nuts compared to the dynamic effect that eliminating corporate income tax will have on economic development and job creation.

We don't need a CBO score to understand the economic effect of eliminating corporate income tax. Other nations have been cutting their tax rates to lure our corporations, facilities, and

---

jobs from us for decades. If our 35% rate is enough to chase jobs to a 25% country, think about what our 0% rate will do to bring jobs here – and I mean jobs by the millions.

Thousands of Americans leave high tax states for low tax states every day; economics works the same way for countries, and we should aim to be the Tennessee of the G-20. Who would have ever guessed we might actually fill all those industrial parks?

The number of jobs created will not just be big; it will be Joe Biden big – and not a moment too soon for the millions of Americans still unemployed and underemployed.

In case you missed it, the Federal Reserve recently estimated it will be years – years, mind you – before the economy just gets back to where it was before the big dump and the unemployment rate falls back under 6%. There is no reason to wait years just so President Obama can finally learn how wrong he is; we can put ourselves back to work right now and let him figure it out for himself later.

More jobs beget more jobs as people work, save, spend, and invest. Eliminating the corporate income tax will reverse our death spiral of higher taxes, more government spending, increasing unemployment, and corporate disinvestment in one fell swoop. The economic vortex is a drain in one direction, and an updraft in the other. Is there an easier or faster way to change direction and initiate the updraft than to eliminate corporate income tax? Let's hear it, and not from Ben Bernanke.

But what about the corporations who depend on those tax subsidies to survive, you may ask? They will either adapt or they will fail, and good riddance to those that fail. If a firm is not economically viable without a subsidy, it is not economically viable. Whole industries will be rationalized and economic efficiency will rule. Free markets – unlike the Minnesota Vikings – do not keep funneling limited resources into obsolete and underperforming technologies year after year.

And economic efficiency, not government subsidy, is the key to our prosperity. It is ridiculous to expect free markets to operate properly with over 1,800 federal interventions managed by people with no business sense. 50% of Americans are of below-average intelligence, and there is no reason to believe that the lure of regularly updated cubicle furniture and two extra holidays per year attracts the upper half into government service.

Until such time as comprehensive tax reform gives us FairTax (my personal preference) or a universal flat tax (acceptable, too), elimination of the corporate income tax is the fastest and most practical economic stimulus we can employ. The bill could be written on a page and passed in a day.

Not convinced yet? Then ponder this: big business, big labor, and big government will join forces to oppose it with all their might. The Defense rests, your Honor.

Not Evil, Just Dyslexic

Here, apparently, is our President's dyslexic interpretation of the 4th amendment: it is unconstitutional for an Arizona cop with probable cause to ask for ID from a guy who just knocked off a liquor store, but it is ok for the TSA at Phoenix airport to reach under a nun's skirt to see if there might be anything interesting up there.

Exactly wrong. The 4th amendment to the Constitution protects citizens (that would be American citizens) from unwarranted searches (that would be searches without probable cause) by government officials (that would be employees of the government, like TSA). It *does not* protect the federal government (that would be INS and ICE) from states (say, Arizona) or the people (that would be us clingers, tea partiers, and voters).

And it is not just the 4th amendment that liberals have stood on end; the 2nd, 1st, 9th, 10th and the enumerated powers in Article I, Section 8 have all been beaten, twisted, hacked and tortured until their original meanings have been turned upside down. The current outrageous TSA fondling episodes are not the most egregious of the left's bold tyrannies; they are simply the hardest to ignore.

For decades, the left has made an industry of fabricating victims, inventing oppressors, and exaggerating the consequences of fictional injustices. Maybe they have played make-believe for so long that they can no longer distinguish between real and imagined rights. Perhaps they have water-boarded the language for so long the can no longer discern the plain meaning of words. Maybe they have lost the ability to recognize tyranny, even when it tweaks their nards or microwaves their inner organs.

Or maybe, just maybe, they have a learning disability - Constitutional Dyslexia – that drives otherwise bright people to get our nation's founding principles back-asswards. Let's give them the benefit of the doubt, and assume they are not evil, just dyslexic. If you or someone you love is suffering from CD, simply repeat after me:

We are not free because we are rich; we are rich because we are free.

We do not need government's permission to act; it needs ours.

We do not receive our rights from government; it receives its authorities from us.

Individual persons create wealth; government can only create money.

We are not created equally; we are created equal.

These are not difficult concepts to grasp; most of us got the drift in high school civics class, despite the distractions of sports, girls, and cars. Yet the statists who run our government and teach in our public schools clearly *don't* get the drift. They have an inverted understanding of the unique relationship ordained between Americans and our government; they confuse the private right to pursue our happiness with the public obligation to purchase theirs.

They do not appreciate the reason that we rose from obscurity to become the greatest nation in the history of the world - freedom. It was freedom that did that. A collection of ordinary persons became an extraordinary people when they were liberated from government interference in economic and personal exchange. How can such a simple truth be so difficult for each generation to accept?

Freedom is the natural state of mankind. Our Creator did not endow us with free will - a gift so precious it was denied to the angels – to have us surrender it to the petty demands of a servant government run amok; a government whose sole purpose is to protect our natural and inalienable rights.

Our government derives its legitimacy from the Constitution by which it came into being; it has no moral authority when it colors outside the lines. And our political dyslexics in both parties have been coloring way outside the lines for many decades now; taking us to the brink of ruin with their social engineering experiments, foreign policy adventurism, and unsound economic theories.

The government they have laid upon us can not realistically be reformed; it must be dismantled, shrunk to size, reduced in scope, de-funded and de-fanged, and returned to its constitutional mission of protecting individual rights and property against force and fraud. We will not return to prosperity until we have tamed the beast that is devouring us.

Returning government to its rightful place is the non-negotiable demand of the liberty movement - the coalition of purpose that has unified conservatives, libertarians, constitutionalists, tea partiers, and sovereign individuals from across the political spectrum to speak with one voice.

A voice whose clear and powerful message is: "leave us alone".

Conspiracy Theory

What a disappointment. Nearly half a million top-secret stolen messages released by WikiLeaks this year and not one smoking gun for the Bindenburg, Illuminati, NWO, Tri-lateral commission, CFR, 9/11 truth, birth certificate, or freemason theorists.

With no disrespect to those who hold to such views, I'm sticking with my original conspiracy theory - government incompetence. The ineptitude, arrogance, and ideological zealotry of the political class are sufficient to explain nearly every insult and injury visited upon mankind by any government entity. The fools who are running us amok are plainly visible, so let's not make this harder than it has to be.

Private actors would have no need for secrecy or collusion to defeat a framework of order and control constructed by idiots – witness the damage George Soros has done on his own - and if the documents just released by WikiLeaks reveal nothing else, they remind us that world leaders are, for the most part, nimrods.

Conspiracy theorists have always had two fundamental problems with their assertion that the world is run by secret societies – the secret part, and the society part. Here is my problem with the "secret" part: we can name them. And even open-minded skeptics like me find it inconceivable that operations of the size and scope of, say, an inside-job 9/11 could be kept secret for over a decade when hundreds of thousands of people would have to be involved logistically to pull it off. That would be hundreds of thousands of low-paid government workers who hate George W. Bush and would be instantly rich and famous if they spilled the beans. I just can't get there.

What did we just witness this week? The world's most secure and most secret communications – diplomatic cables – were stolen by a private-first-class and published by a broke Austrian nerd on the lamb. And the Illuminati could not stop these two? This little Assange fellow would give a kidney to publish the smoking gun for a 9/11 false flag operation, yet not one email, not one cable, not one dollar of hush money, not one private-first-class or one rent-a-jihad turns up in his mother lode of post-Bush gossip-mongering. Nothing - just like WMD in Iraq.

"Might have" is not "did". Questions are not answers, and the WikiLeaks dump provided no answers – not to 9/11, or Kenyan birth certificates, or any other subject of amped-up speculation that is so tempting to accept, if for no other reason that to provide an alternative to the unsatisfying explanation that crazy stuff happens.

But let's recall that a sitting President was nearly brought down because just *two* people – one whose Presidency depended on it, and the other whose life depended on it – could not keep a secret of the most intimate sort. A ruthless global cabal capable of collapsing the world's financial system could not manage to snuff out one chubby intern? Was there kryptonite in those knee pads? Some EMI jammers in the thong that foiled the black helicopters and ninja assassins' GPS? The living Monica proves Vince Foster's death really was a suicide, as much as I would like to doubt it.

And here is the problem with the "society" part: megalomaniacs do not play nice with the other children. WikiLeaks confirms. With all the troubles in the world, Hillary Clinton is radar-locked on digging dirt on her colleagues; ordering career diplomats to dumpster-dive and get credit card numbers to see if some U.N. Ambassador from whatsit-stan is buying toys from Adam and Eve.

She wants to know if Evo Morales likes her, what medicine Argentina's President is taking for anxiety, whether Karzai uses Grecian formula, who's got girlfriends, and who has boyfriends. What is this – the eighth grade? Supposedly, these folks are on the same team – infiltrators inserted by the puppet masters, recall - and yet their only team accomplishment is mutual trash-talk behind each others' backs.

If this is diplomacy – the second to last resort - it is no wonder that we keep stumbling headlong into the last resort – war. While the latest pile of poo dumped into the ether by WikiLeaks provides no evidence of any New World Order, it adds a mountain of new evidence that the incompetent political class -

the Old World Order – remains firmly entrenched from Buenos Aires to Beijing, from Mumbai to Moscow.

Personally, I am conflicted about the whole WikiLeaks phenomenon – in a world where diplomats can not speak in confidence, guns will do the talking. On the other hand, we will never know how much we are being lied to if we take the liars' word for it. The hero or villain of the WikiLeaks disclosures, depending on your point of view, is a self-promoting jerk and sport rapist; even Oliver Stone won't make us like this guy when the inevitable movie comes out. Whatever you think of the whole deal, I wouldn't argue; this sort of ambivalence is thankfully rare.

In the end, I have concluded WikiLeaks is just clutter, enough low-grade ammo to get both the neo-cons and takes-a-village socialists all sweaty playing gotcha for the next few weeks on Fox and NPR, respectively. Did you learn anything you didn't already know or suspect? Me neither. Politicians scheme and lie; no Pulitzer there.

And while we were diverted by the big yawn, BernankeLeaks fessed up to giving $9 trillion to his bankster buddies, and GeithnerLeaks let on that he will back the Euro-doof's bond bailout with our tax dollars. Thankfully, someone already invented the word that fits between "un" and "believable" or we would have to come up with one now under duress. Back to my point; there is no need to theorize complex hidden conspiracies when the d-bags are screwing us out in the open and right before our very eyes.

So my libertarian told-you-so takeaway from Cable-Gate is this: Don't let these people run *anything*.

When the founding fathers warned against interventions abroad, this is exactly the kind of trouble they meant for us to avoid. We are now up to our necks in military, political, and financial relationships we can't manage, can't control, and can't afford. We are now joined into complex alliances with bastards we wouldn't let anywhere near our children. WikiLeaks confirms that the leaders of the "international community" could pass for the cast of Celebrity Rehab – a bunch of seriously messed up narcissists whose long-range goal is the next minute of attention they crave.

Don't give it to them. Don't give them war. Don't give them diplomacy. Don't give them climate change. Don't give them trade. Don't give them health care. Don't give them the currency. Don't give them the food supply. Don't give them the energy supply. Don't give them your job. Don't give them your money. Don't give them your guns. Don't give them your Constitution. Don't give them anything important to do.

They can't handle it. They just got their asses handed to them by a guy named Julian...with a notebook computer...from Sweden. Fail.

Quit Suffering

A bright young man noticed my Libertarian Party lapel pin and posed this gotcha question to impress his friends: "so what is your answer to current suffering?" My response: "quit suffering". His friend's analysis of the exchange: "schooled".

"Schooled" may be a bit harsh, but "quit suffering" was certainly not the answer that the first fellow expected. The modern-day debate about poverty has always revolved around what the government should do about it. Government spending on poverty programs is the liberal's unit of measure for public morality. But the truth of the matter is that there is very little the government can do about poverty, except create more of the stuff with bone-headed monetary and fiscal policies.

Fortunately we live in America, where most poverty is avoidable. If we graduate from high school, don't do drugs, don't do crime, get married and stay married, have children (after we are married), and get a job, 99.4% of us will avoid chronic poverty on our own, without any government assistance. That is what the Census Bureau's poverty statistics tell us.

However, if we drop out of high school, we are 3 times as likely to be poor than if we graduate. If we are unmarried with kids, we are 4 times as likely to be poor than if we are married with kids. If we are unemployed, we are 10 times as likely to be poor than if we work. The unemployment rate for felons is over 70%, and it is 100% for burned-out drug zombies.

Which is not to say that you don't have an absolute right to quit school, have kids out of wedlock, get divorced, quit your job, blow your mind, or commit a victimless "crime". You do, you do, you most certainly do. You just have no right to pass the consequences of your own actions off to your neighbors. And we are not obligated to pick up your tab. Freedom is a Dutch Treat lifestyle.

People don't do all those things because they are poor; people are poor because they do all those things. In the main, poverty is a choice. Ok, rich liberals, feel free to go berserk now if it will make you feel better about yourselves. But this isn't about you;

it is about helping people actually get *out* of poverty. There is no reason for able people to be "trapped" in perpetual poverty, as some basic math will illustrate:

According to the Labor Department, the poverty threshold for a family of four (two adults, two children) is $21,756. If mom and dad work even minimum wage jobs, household income will be $30,160 or 138% of the poverty threshold. And dad can work another part time job (I'm old fashioned that way), raising the family income to $37,700 at minimum wage. Get OJT, take continuing education courses, get promoted, and wages will increase in proportion to the value added - at just $10/hr family income is $52,000 when both parents work a combined 2.5 jobs.

Don't tell me it can't be done. I did it. And I did it because it sucked to be poor, not because a liberal cared about me. Millions of Americans fall down and get back up again each year without waiting for the government to fix our problems at someone else's expense. Poverty statistics show that up until 2008, most poverty was episodic – i.e. lasting a couple months – typically caused by a job loss, domestic breakup, catastrophic medical event, or similar visitation of bad times.

Yes, it is hard work to quit suffering; and so what - life is hard for everybody. Two income families are the norm nowadays. Millions of small business owners would love to only work 60 hours. Most people have worked two or three jobs when we had to, and went back to school so we would not have to do that forever. Many of us work at jobs we don't like. Staying married is hard work, too, and so is taking a pass on the bong so we can pass our drug tests. Intemperance is a lot easier and a whole lot more fun than restraint, but restraint is what keeps us out of jail, on the job, and out of poverty.

The young man should have asked himself: what is the government's answer to current suffering? Answer: more suffering. Five decades and a few trillion dollars into the war on poverty, poverty is winning; the current poverty rate is *higher* than when we gave the socialists their head in 1965. As long as there are government poverty programs, there will be sufficient numbers of poor people to justify them; recipients are a necessary ingredient of the welfare state.

CAPITALISTA!

This week's tax compromise extends "temporary" unemployment insurance benefits out to three years. Three years! In any of the five previous recessions going back to 1970, the median length of unemployment did not reach three months. When state unemployment insurance premiums skyrocket next year, it will be fun to watch President Obama try to figure out whose butt to kick.

Government does not own the franchise on morality. Politicians do not help poor people when they blame their plight on others. Government schools *create* poverty by leaving students unprepared for the world of work and unacquainted with free markets. Welfare encourages chronic poverty, except for the government workers it overpays to fill out useless forms for each other to file. Our drug laws create legions of felons unnecessarily. A century of collectivist social engineering has decimated the nuclear family and desecrated the ideal of self-reliance. The government's track record is deplorable - the more it spends, the more it harms.

It doesn't take a village to raise a child; it takes a mom and a dad and a church of your choice. The anecdote for poverty is liberty, not government; liberty is the absence of government in choice. Poverty is not overcome by social consciousness; it is only defeated by individual responsibility. Our young people need to learn that poverty is avoidable and need to be taught how to avoid it: graduate, get a job, get married and stay married, have kids, don't do drugs, don't do crimes, and don't look to government to solve your problems.

Quit suffering. It is a choice, not a life sentence.

Tri-partisanship

Once is an anomaly, twice is a coincidence, and three times is a trend. For three straight election cycles now, a political Party was defeated by a coalition of two principled Philosophies. Welcome to the tri-partisan world.

The two political parties – Democrat and Republican – have been leaking oil for some time now; they have devolved into marketing vehicles that package candidates to fit advertising strategies preferred by their donor benefactors. Not so long ago, parties could elect candidates on their own, but neither one has the mass to accomplish that anymore. And besides, the citizenry has moved past party affiliation.

Americans prefer to identify with one of three principled political philosophies – liberal, conservative, and libertarian. Republicans learned the difference between "Republican" and "conservative" from George W. Bush and Tom DeLay. Democrats learned the difference between "Democrat" and "liberal" when Democrat Hillary Clinton's coronation was derailed by liberal Barack Obama in the 2008 primaries.

In the tri-partisan sphere, it takes a coalition of two of the three principled political philosophies to move the needle on any substantive issue. We libertarians are small in comparison to liberals or conservatives, but recall that Sandra Day O'Conner made up only 11% of the Supreme Court when she cast the deciding votes in a long string of very important 5-4 decisions.

Think about the past three election cycles in terms of two parties and they appear to be senseless flailing; but think in terms of principled tri-partisanship and they make perfect sense.

In 2006, liberals ran against the Party of Bush on three issues: war, deficit spending, and earmarks. Libertarians joined with them and Republicans went down in flames. In 2008, libertarians (and a good many conservatives) sat on our hands after the Republican Party disrespected our man Ron Raul and nominated John McCain; and the Republicans got punished again. In 2010, libertarians enthusiastically joined with conservatives to rout the Democrat Party and establish the tea party movement.

In three straight cycles, two principled philosophies joined forces to defeat one of the political parties; and in all three cycles, libertarians were the swing vote. But are any of the leading Republican candidates for 2012 working to build upon the conservative/libertarian coalition that fueled the tea parties and re-shaped Congress? No, they are not; and that is why I do not believe our next President is known to the nation yet, just as Barack Obama was unknown to us in 2007.

But that election is far off, and it will not be easy to reach compromise in Washington for the next two years, since liberals, conservatives, and libertarians have completely different ideas about what government should be and why we even need it in the first place.

Liberals see government as a kindly crossing guard, there to help groups of needy little citizens overcome barriers and avoid danger. Conservatives view government as a stern magistrate, upholding standards, promoting values and traditions, interpreting timeless rules, and punishing outliers. Libertarians view government as those maniac cops that beat the crap out of Rodney King.

Each of these three avatars is grounded in an element of truth; the rule of law observed from three different vantage points. This makes it hard for us to communicate and work together.

When liberals advocate government expansion, we libertarians brace for more beatings. When we propose less government, liberals envision unemployed crossing guards and children huddled on the corner, unable to make it home in time to pee. Conservatives just want to know how much it will cost to pay off the magistrate so future disputes settle in their favor.

I understand tri-partisanship perfectly; I grew up in a home with three boys. It was always two brothers against one, but never the same two or the same one twice in a row. And that is how this nation will go forward in the tri-partisan world – two against one with liberals, conservatives, and libertarians forming principled alliances around specific issues as they arise, and uniting only if credible external threats to the nation arise.

Tri-partisanship will mean gridlock for the next two years in Washington; the crossing guards will weep, the magistrates will grind their teeth, and us libertarians will be happy that the beatings have stopped, if only temporarily.

Eventually, someone will get serious about solving our nation's problems, but until that day comes, gridlock is a blessing.

Math Whiz

This week we learned that American teens have fallen to the #24 rank in national math proficiency; or maybe it was #25, counting that high is, like, way hard. The good news here is that our shortage of math whizzes assures us an ample supply of potential qualified Fed Chairmen and Senators from Massachusetts.

Appearing on NBC Meet The Press recently to argue for raising taxes and extending unemployment benefits, Sen. John Kerry explained that every dollar spent on unemployment benefits generated $1.60 of economic growth. I thought maybe he misspoke, but he said it twice more. And he said it with a straight face, as certain about his economic calculations as the day he proposed to the Ketchup lady.

Have you ever heard anything less believable from a grown-up person who is not drunk and begging an ex-spouse to take them back? Where does that other 60¢ come from, your Heinz-ness? Do we put our unemployment dollar under the pillow and wait for the Tooth Fairy to apply the Keynesian multiplier? Do you deliver it to us personally in your tax-evading, registered-in-Connecticut yacht? It's humiliation enough that you lost to George W. Bush; you don't need to keep reminding us why.

Try Kerry's whacky economic theory out for yourself at the Wal-Mart - buy something priced at $1.59 and give the clerk a one-dollar bill. When she gives you that are-you-high-or-just-slow look, just tell her it's ok, this dollar is special – it came from unemployment. When she asks where on earth you got such a stupid idea, point to that new Big Sis Janet Napolitano video and say, "her guy said so; and hey - why are you being so suspicious about economics, anyway? You some kind of jee-had? Manager! Manager!" That should knock the boring off a Saturday night.

Senator Kerry was on a roll that Sunday; he went on to further enlighten us that if we keep our money, that same dollar will only generate 30¢ of economic growth; that's why they have to tax it, you see. Really? And where, pray tell, does the other 70¢ go off to? Does it evaporate? Spontaneous combustion? And does this mean they have to give us 70¢ change now at the

Dollar Store? Because I use my own money there. And answer me this, Senator: how come when the Fed turns a dollar into 30¢ you call it Quantitative Easing, but if we do it somehow by keeping what we earned (humor me, people) you call it greed?

According to Senator Kerry, if we increase taxes *and* we extend unemployment benefits, then we will be $1.30 to the good, collecting both the 60 and the 70 cents. Obama, Pelosi, Krugman, Reid, and the whole socialist cast of DC's Dancing with the Dolts think this way. By the way, Senator Kerry is not just any Senator; he is Chairman of the Senate Small Business Committee, which explains why small businesses keep getting kicked in the groin every time a bill passes in Washington.

Where the 60¢ came from and where the 70¢ went to would both have been really good questions for MTP host David Gregory to ask; but he just sat there panting and wagging his tail and waiting for a Greenie. I would have asked Mr. Kerry the more obvious question: "Isn't hard to drive with your head up there?" Wouldn't you just love to guest host one of those Sunday shows for an episode? Republican or Democrat, I don't care, just send over one of those blow-dried peacocks and let me sweat 'em for an hour strapped to a polygraph. Emmy.

And where was the senior Senator from Massachusetts all the while that loopy deficit commission was sucking up our tax dollars on $40 Waldorf salads at the Ritz? Who knew it could be this easy: just pay $10 trillion in unemployment benefits and that Kerry multiplier magically creates another $6 trillion to pay down the debt. What the hell, let's go $20 trillion and be debt-free for Christmas; nobody works and we all have plenty of time to enjoy the holidays with our families.

And that, apparently, is no problem, because our other resident math whiz, Fed Chairman Ben Bernanke, assured us that same Sunday evening on CBS 60 Minutes that he it does not inflate the money supply when he adds $600 billion to it out of thin air. Really? Hot damn – then just print up $32 trillion more, buy $20 trillion of T-bills so Kerry can pay us all not to work, and then use the other $12 trillion (the 1.60 force multiplier) to pay off the national debt. Kerry and Bernanke on the same Sunday – thank God neither of them was scoring the Packer game we would never know who won. Probably Manchester United.

CAPITALISTA!

I had the good fortune not long ago to spend a couple of days with Dr. Arthur Laffer, the internationally acclaimed economist, and one of the smartest people I have ever met. I asked him his opinion of the Keynesian multiplier theory (like Kerry's $1.60). He replied that it is arithmetic, not economics. Concise.

Senator Kerry made his money the old fashioned way; he married it, in the person of heiress Teresa Heinz. Unfortunately, the supply of rich widows and widowers of prematurely deceased capitalists is limited, as is the number of "heiress" positions available, so nearly all of those 15 year-olds who just tested so poorly in math, reading, and science are going to have to survive on their own poorly educated wits while competing head-on against the gonzo-capitalist math-monsters from Shanghai.

They like President Obama over in Shanghai, because, as one student explained to me recently, "his policies are good for China". She was the same girl who wished she could live in America, where "you can become rich because you are free". Our kids aren't learning that here, which makes them less likely to be either rich or free. Pity.

Is there a better poster boy for liberal hypocrisy than Senator Kerry? According to Wikipedia, the Kerrys' combined net worth is estimated to be $1.2 billion. They own 5 homes valued at more than $5 million each. Senator Kerry moors his yacht in Connecticut to avoid paying Massachusetts taxes on it. And according to their most recently released income tax data, the Kerrys' paid an effective federal income tax rate of only 12%. Isn't that precious – 12 whole percentage points.

These are the people who think *you* don't pay enough taxes. These are the people who call *you* greedy for wanting keeping your top marginal rate at 35%, while they pay 12%.

They call *you* unpatriotic for wanting to pass your estate on to your children, while they live large off of tax-sheltered family trusts for generations. Trusts that have been replenished by the trillions of dollars Ben Bernanke and the Fed continue to pump into their too-connected-to-fail member banks. They don't mind raising tax rates, because they have no intention of ever paying them.

I'm no math whiz either, but I can count to two, and the second word is "off". Here's my idea for a compromise on tax rates this year: nobody gets a tax increase until every single one of these a-hole Congressmen and Senators actually *pays* the top marginal rate they piss-and-moan about incessantly.

January can't come too soon.

Trainiacs

When I was nine years old and didn't get the train I wanted for Christmas, I pouted for half a day. Here in Wisconsin, it has been six weeks since the November election that killed high speed rail, and our trainiacs are still pouting.

For the benefit of readers around the world, our former (and very unpopular) Governor skirted the law and bought some train cars over in Spain; then he fetched some federal stimulus money to run a high-speed rail line between our two biggest cities, Madison and Milwaukee, a distance of 72 miles. The $850 million project became a central campaign issue in the gubernatorial race this year, and anti-train Republican candidate Scott Walker won.

The politics of high speed rail is predictable: liberals and Democrats love public transportation, while conservatives and Republicans don't. Libertarians never get past the "public" part to even get to the thing that other two are fussing about – transportation, housing, education, television, fill-in-the-blank.

In November, Wisconsin flipped from blue to red everywhere - Governor, Senator, both houses of the state legislature, and our D.C. Congressional delegation. Hello Governor Walker, goodbye train.

And the trainiacs went berserk. Then Walker asked DOT to use the money they would have spent on HSR to repair their crumbling roads and bridges in our state. And the trainiacs went berserk. When the Obama administration said no, the anti-trainiacs went berserk. The feds said they would build the train here whether Wisconsin wanted it or not. The anti-trainiacs went berserk. Walker said no, actually, you won't, and the trainiacs went berserk.

Finally, Obama took back the stimulus money from Wisconsin and gave it to California, and trainiacs went into a permanent state of berserkitude. Some day, when a Wisconsin bridge collapses on top of a bus full of special needs children, I would like all my liberal and trainiac friends to remember who killed those kids.

But the inconsolable and still berserk trainiacs are not thinking about special needs children right now. I feel for them; I was crushed too when I didn't get my train for Christmas. But if it's any consolation, here is the proof that this rail project was a horrible idea: California jumped at it. Kind of like worrying if you did the right thing breaking up with your hot-but-possibly-crazy girlfriend until you read that she is now living with Charlie Sheen. We dodged a bullet not marrying high speed rail; let Charlie have her.

The real issue was never the train; we all like trains, especially the fast ones. It was – and is – all about who pays to ride it. The proposed fare for a one-way ticket was $32; but that is only what the *rider* would pay. The non-riding taxpayer would pick up the other $68 of the $100 actual cost per trip. High speed rail is the literal incarnation of the metaphorical free ride – the fraud upon which modern liberalism is based. The more obvious fraud of this HSR project is the "high speed" part – our train was going to trundle along at only 57 mph.

But "who pays" should be the start and the end of the legitimate debate over Wisconsin's HSR. If a Milwaukee lawyer wants to read Investor's Business Daily and drink a Chivas on his way to lobby Madison lawmakers for a tax loophole on behalf of a client, fine; but why should a waitress in Woodruff be forced to buy his ticket? Should we also stick her with 2/3 of his cab fare to get from the train station to the lobby of the hotel where he will drop off the campaign cash and grab a room for the afternoon? Why not make her pay for all of his rides?

Train mania began in the 1960's and 70's when American hippies traveled around Europe to find themselves – and girls and dope – and discovered the EuroRail Pass with its flat-fee unlimited ridership. For the past 40 years, trainiacs and pandering politicians have been pushing high-speed and light rail projects in the U.S. and for 40 years they all come up a cropper, as they just did in Wisconsin. The emergency stop cord always gets yanked at the ballot box – thankfully, there are more waitresses who don't want to pay someone else's fare than there are lawyers who think the world owes them a free ride. My libertarian solution for Wisconsin's pouting trainiacs is to buck up and build the blasted thing themselves.

CAPITALISTA!

1,004,257 Wisconsinites voted against Mr. Walker and his promise to cancel the HSR project. If each of them would invest just $847 in The People's Train they could have the object of their desire - at least that is what the DOT said the thing would cost to build. Entrepreneurs invest their whole life savings into the things they care passionately about, so it is not unreasonable to ask trainiacs to come up with $847.

And they would not just have a train; they would *own* the train. They can run it however they see fit. They can set their own fares – progressive fares based on income, one would hope. They can add solar panels and windmills, pour ethanol and bio-fuel into the diesel tanks, install fluorescent dairy queen bulbs everywhere, and get rid of that nasty carbon-emitting air-conditioning and heating of the cabins.

They could make everyone go through the security porno scanner *and* feel you up before you get on their train. Hope and Change, Grope and Trains, whatever. They could pay those sky-high corporate tax rates they like so much, donate profits to NPR instead of receiving dividends, and hire all the nation's unemployed railroad workers whether they need them or not. They can ban smoking, e-smoking, talking about smoking, thinking about smoking, texting, guns, raw milk, happy meals, SUV's, Weber grills, home-grown foods, facebook, and Rush Limbaugh on their trains.

They can set racial quotas and diversity-train (no pun intended) people for hours a day; they can make employees join not just one union but two or three, each of which pays all of their insurance and gives them a fabulous pension after 10 years of working. Hell, let's make the riders join a union, too; and make them all wear helmets while we are at it. Install airbags in every seat and a video screen with Janet Napolitano begging you to snitch on fellow passengers over and over again for the whole duration of the trip – especially the folks with Ron Paul stickers or a Gadsden flag hat.

And when the project cost comes in $200-400 million higher than DOT said it would (which is what independent estimates predict), the *owners* would naturally have to pick up that tab. And *owners* pay for the tens of millions in operating losses each year that the train will generate at its predicted 25% occupancy.

And *owners* would settle the lawsuits over disturbing the pond scum near the tracks if someone finds an endangered beetle within 100 miles. And *owners* pay for the work comp claims, unemployment claims, fees and licenses, discrimination claims, and all the slip-n-trip lawsuits, like when our drunken lawyer friend passes out and hits his head. And when the EPA doubles energy costs, *owners* can eat it instead of passing it on to their customers, like the bad capitalists' corporations do. And owners can sell their $847 shares of People's Rail Incorporated at market price, which would be zero within a few minutes of its creation. Owners can lose *everything.*

So, what do you say, trainiacs? Doesn't this sound like a fabulous investment opportunity to you? Wouldn't you gladly pay $847 to own it, thousands more each year to operate it and $200 for each round trip fare when you ride it, watching the $35 fare buses and $12 of gasoline cars go speeding by you on the interstate, while your investment turns to mush at very high speeds?

I didn't think so. And neither would the taxpayers of Wisconsin; that is why you aren't getting your train for Christmas. Quit pouting and enjoy the holidays.

Who Owns You?

The libertarian philosophy can be condensed to its essence: we are all obligated to live honestly, without initiating force or fraud upon another human being. And that is my Christmas wish for all who follow Dr. Tim's Moment Of Clarity – an honest life free from force or fraud.

The libertarian's political ambition is to impose the smallest government footprint capable of enforcing this obligation upon all who operate within its domain. Government, by its nature, is organized force; everything a government does is achieved through coercion. Laws compel individuals to obey; failure to comply results in deprivation of economic liberty (fines, confiscation) or personal liberty (prison). Fraud – falsifying, misleading, and materially misrepresenting for gain – is the modus operandi of the partisan politicians who control government and determine the purposes to which its force will be applied.

The State is both the government (force) and the partisans (fraud) who control it. Libertarians view the State as the enemy of liberty; it is a verdict directed by history. And we, quite proudly, are enemies of the State. Libertarians oppose any political philosophy, party, person, or initiative that seeks to expand the power of the State at the expense of individual liberty. We stand with all who will defend individual rights, and we stand against any who seek to impose collective privilege.

However, libertarians are not anarchists, and we recognize that a certain amount of liberty must be ceded to government to protect our remaining liberties from the aggression of others. We do not advocate abolition of courts, defensive armed forces, law enforcement agencies, legislatures, and the whole of the bureaucracy; our non-negotiable demand is merely that they abide by the constraints of the Constitution from which their authority is derived. We do not advocate lawlessness; we advocate less laws.

Economic liberty and personal liberty are two sides of the same coin. You cannot pretend to give away the heads and keep the tails. Each dollar confiscated by the State is one dollar that you are not free to use according to your own conscience and beliefs. It is one unit of your labor - your person – that has become the property of someone else. You are *not* property. You are not chattel to be looted by the State on behalf of a temporary electoral majority; you are a self-sovereign person, a child of God.

Principled conservatives and libertarians are natural allies in matters of economic liberty – taxes, trade, fiscal discipline, monetary policy, property rights, regulation, employment, market independence, etc. Principled liberals and libertarians are natural allies in matters of personal liberty – crime and punishment, lifestyle choices, equal rights, first amendment protections, religious tolerance, anti-discrimination, immigration, censorship, military conscription, and the like.

But socialists and libertarians have no mutual interests, and no principles to share; we are natural adversaries. Whether the socialists are right-wing or left-wing, or operate under the Democrat or Republican brands is immaterial. Libertarians do not accept the Statists' partisan notion of "public good" that justifies any and all use of force to expand the State at the expense of individual liberty. Collectivism is incompatible with full and equal personhood.

Who owns you? This is the fundamental question that libertarians challenge you to answer for yourself – the one that separates the collectivist from the individualist.

We believe that each of us completely owns our person, the fruits of our labors, and the consequences of our actions. The libertarian notion of *volition* is the secular understanding of the religious concept of *free will*. You and you alone are entitled to your life, liberty, and property; no one else on this earth has a superior claim on it, as it was gifted to you by a Higher Power. You are not obligated to sacrifice yourself on demand of another. Greed does not attach to those who refuse to be sacrificed; rather it is the defining characteristic of those who demand sacrifice from others.

Libertarians are non-interventionists at home and abroad. We believe that undeclared wars are unjust, and that world government is unjustifiable. We believe that voluntary exchange

– free market capitalism – is the only moral basis for economic transactions between equal and self-sovereign people. Government is an at-will employee of its citizens - subordinate and contingent, and subject to nullification when it refuses to abide by its lawful constraints.

Our duty to each other is simply not to aggress; to live in peace and to respect the right of every other person to do the same. But if force or fraud is perpetrated against us, it is our duty to defend ourselves and the inalienable rights which were endowed to us by our Creator. Failing to do so would devalue the gift, dishonor the Giver, and disinherit generations to whom we owe the passing of liberty's fullness. Charity born of volition blesses the giver; conscription is the preening of a tyrant.

Liberty is the absence of government in choice, government is the absence of liberty in choice, and tyranny is the absence of choice in government. Once the unifying principles upon which this nation was founded, these tenets are now considered radical – that is how far down F.A. Hayek's Road To Serfdom the socialists have marched us over the past century. Radical it is, then. We libertarians refuse to complete the journey; we choose to turn back and walk to the light of liberty, and we hope you will choose to follow.

Merry Christmas from Dr. Tim. Thanks for reading my posts, buying the book, and coming to hear me speak. And thanks for everything *you* do to advance the cause of liberty. Now enjoy the holidays with your families and friends and give all this political fussing a rest for a few days. That's what I'm going to do.

A More Perfect Union

The problem with compulsory unionization is simple enough: it is incompatible with a commitment to liberty and equal rights. Each of us has the right to form a union and bargain collectively; and each of us has the equal right to work union-free. The Constitution does not select one over the other.

The absurdity of the unionists' demand for compulsory and collective workplace privilege becomes obvious when it is extended to any other third party: Should only members of the KKK hold government jobs? Should only Lutherans be permitted to teach your children? Should you be forced to join the NRA to keep your job and should your employer be forced to collect your membership dues? Should we have a federal agency devoted to increasing membership in the Crips? Should NOW membership be imposed in your workplace without a vote through Card Check? Should your wages be confiscated to fund the political campaigns of Freemasons?

There is only one way to guarantee the equal protection of the Constitution for everyone in the workplace - Right To Work.

In the 22 states that have already enacted RTW protections for their citizens, workers are free to join or not join a union as they see fit, and employers are not obligated to confiscate union dues from worker's pay. Worker Choice is not merely an economic policy; it is a matter of fundamental liberty that requires no defense. Humans must produce to live; the right to work is inseparable from the rights to life, liberty, and the pursuit of happiness.

Opponents of Right To Work must defend the indefensible proposition that you do *not* have the right to work. They must convince you that *they* have the right to prevent you from working; that *they* can force you to join their organization against your will, and dictate the terms of your employment. They must insist that *they* are entitled to force your employer to collect their dues without compensation for the service, and to discipline insurgent members on their behalf.

CAPITALISTA!

They believe their right of coercion is superior to your right not to be coerced. Where do they discover this right to coerce your fellow citizens? Show it to me. Is it found in the Constitution, the Bible, Koran, in the teachings of any prophet, or in the writings of any great philosopher? No, it is not.

What is their objection to open-shop rules, where employees are free to bargain collectively or not in their work place? If the union adds value, as it claims, employees will see this first hand and readily join. If union labor is superior, as it claims, employers will gladly choose to employ more of it. If unionism were in everyone's best interest, as it claims, then everyone will choose it enthusiastically.

In fact, if unions would *guarantee* the quality, safety, and availability of their workforce, employers would have a powerful incentive to choose union labor exclusively. The more perfect union is the one which individuals are free to choose, not forced to join. If liberty offends, then let the unionists be offended.

But open-shop will never be acceptable to the unions, or their wholly owned subsidiary, the Democrat Party. Voluntary unionism is rejected by unionists for the same reason Muslim fundamentalists reject voluntary marriage - both the unionist and the lousy husband know that they could never win affection in competition, so they force subjugation instead. The suffering of others is of no concern to those lack empathy. Mob rule makes perfect sense to the mob.

Unions are acutely aware that their survival is completely dependent on State enforcement of their workplace monopoly. And like any monopoly, decades of insulation from choice and competition has produced institutional pathologies that have corrupted unionism from a once-worthy cause into a destructive force in the workplace. Where unions thrive, jobs die.

The deadly combination of unsustainable compensation growth and work-rule rigidity has destroyed whole industries in America - shipbuilding, textiles, appliances, furniture, electronics, steel, mining, automobiles, railroads, foundry, shoes, leather goods, airlines, and musical instruments come immediately to mind. Rejected by over 90% of workers in the private sector, unions have turned to organizing government and education – bankrupting the former and debasing the latter.

By contrast, the most vibrant economic sector over the past three decades – the tech sector – is the least unionized, the least regulated, the least bound by licensure, the least impacted by government meddling, the least subsidized, the least protected and the least bound by traditional labor relations tenets. This is no accident.

Prosperity is the gift of individual liberty, and bankruptcy is the reward for collective mediocrity; this is the lesson of economic history.

While prosperity cannot be legislated, the conditions that bring it about most certainly can be. Here in Wisconsin, the control of state government was taken away from liberal Democrats and given over to conservative Republicans this past November. The liberty coalition that flipped this state did not do so to win a sporting contest for a political party. We did so to change our economic trajectory and reaffirm our commitment to equal rights.

Do the Republicans understand why they were given back the reins of government in the industrial heartland? They can show us by enacting Right To Work – and not a moment too soon when they do.

Relentless

Congressional sessions have become like NBA games: they pose, sleepwalk, and talk smack for most of it and then play like they mean it for the last five minutes.

So in a flurry of activity that included every manner of legislative maneuver except for actually reading any of the bills that they passed, our 111th Congress wrapped up its lame duck session by passing a new arms treaty, an extension – sort of - of the Bush tax cuts, unemployment benefit extension, emergency funding to keep the government going a couple more weeks, another war supplemental, DADT repeal, and a Food Safety Bill that marks the beginning of the war on gardening.

None of us knows for sure what the impact of any of these laws will be, since the media confined its coverage to the politics of it all – scoring wins and losses for the two parties and handicapping the 2012 Presidential field. It would have been nice to know that we unilaterally gave up missile defense – relying instead on perpetual foreign occupation - *before* the vote on START. Nice work, groupies.

President Obama was quite pleased with himself. Apparently, for reasons that defy human understanding, he believes that the American people punished him at the polls in November for not doing *enough*. And the pundits are hailing Harry Reid as the master tactician, as if we should be grateful to him for passing more unpopular bills that spend more money we don't have by tossing more pork at the outgoing senators we fired in last year's primaries. If the GOP leadership learned anything from the November elections, it was not evident to me in the last days of the session.

But the President and his crew saved their best stuff for Executive Orders, simply bypassing Congress altogether and putting the beat-down on liberty without the bother of securing a vote from those we pay to represent us in such matters.

His FDA decreed we could drink alcohol or caffeine, but not together. His EPA decided it owns CO_2, the stuff we exhale. His Interior Secretary banned drilling in the Gulf. He created a new

Public Health Council to prioritize a list of "lifestyle behavior modifications" for the country. His TSA took it upon itself to give us the porn-pat-stay ultimatum. His NLRB forced contractors to put up new pro-union posters in their lunchrooms. The exceptions he granted to his ObamaCare mandate now outnumber the list of new mandates contained in the bill. And for the coup-de-grace, his FCC ended King Barack's best-year-ever by taking over the Internet.

Relentless – that's what they are.

Relentless like Chuckie, that horror-movie doll who keeps coming after you even though he has been repeatedly and mortally wounded. Special elections, falling poll numbers, primary races, BP spill fiasco, Spanish vacations, adverse court rulings, foreign policy embarrassments, the November shellacking, Charlie Rangel's ethics violations, Juan Williams firing, state laws, Keith Olbermann's suspension, voter intimidation, Climategate, WikiLeaks, ACORN busted – nothing stops our little socialist Chuckies.

Did you have to take over the Internet, you relentless little Chuckies at FCC? The one thing the government couldn't keep up with, the one thing you couldn't control, the one thing you haven't ruined, the one thing that is better now than it used to be, the one thing we still do better than the rest of the world. The one thing that sets us free...from you. Was it so awful for you that we were happy?

And did you have to cut off Texas' energy, you joyless prigs at EPA? The one state that runs budget surpluses. The one state with billions still in their rainy day fund. The one state that never stopped creating jobs. The state that businesses are moving to, not from. The state with no income tax, a part-time legislature, Right To Work, concealed carry; the state that follows the Constitution. Was it just too humiliating to watch Nancy Pelosi's and Barack Obama's home states taxing and regulating themselves into liberal default while Ron Paul's state thrives in liberty?

Speaking of Nancy's home state, how fitting that her own congressional district, San Francisco, was the one to ban Happy Meals. I don't know why they stopped there; just get it over with and ban Happy altogether. Better yet, make happiness a hate crime, since you all hate it so much when anyone is happy without your permission. McDonalds should have thrown a condom in with the Transformers - the little Chuckies would be force-feeding McRibs to third graders and Ronald would be the Grand Marshall in the next parade.

It is difficult for libertarians to imagine the lengths to which statists will go to force-fit society into the mold of their values and beliefs. We lack the coercion gene, the need to be obeyed, and the burning desire to lord over our fellow citizens. We are tolerant to a fault, trusting enlightened self-interest and personal responsibility in matters of human interaction. We respect each person as an equal sovereign; we find the herd model of today's liberal shepherds to be dehumanizing.

I wish our professional nags would be as relentless about reading as they are about telling us what to do. They would learn that Karl Marx ultimately renounced his abolishment of private property rights. They would discover that FDR's Treasury Secretary admitted his Keynesian New Deal economics failed. They would appreciate that the horrors of socialism described by Hayek and Rand were not theorized, but observed first-hand.

They might also notice that the socialist Europe they fantasize over is insolvent, that 30 blue states are bankrupt, that 100 cities are about to default on $2 trillion in municipal bonds, and that the re-financing of the 2009 mortgage bailouts is about to begin at 150 points higher interest, spurring another round of foreclosures and declining property values. They might be aware that China and Russia dropped the U.S. Dollar as bi-lateral trade currency – other nations are not waiting around for us to End The Fed, they are taking matters into their own hands.

But the relentless socialist Chuckies have no time for reading and contemplation; they are too busy lining pockets, banning happiness, taking choice away, legislating conformance, forcing compliance, pandering to voting blocks, manipulating markets, extending foreign occupations, bankrupting the nation, suing the states, stamping out liberty, and congratulating themselves for all the fine work they have done since taking the reigns of Congress in 2007.

But they know better. Perhaps the President's most telling executive branch edict was the quiet decision by the Bureau of Labor Statistics recently to modify the unemployment rate calculation, extending the length of time that unemployed people are still considered in the labor force from two years to five. Don't think they don't know what lies in store for us. They know.

Their recession is relentless, their assault on our liberties is relentless, their foreign interventions are relentless, and their lust for power is relentless. This month a whole crop of newly elected representatives will get the chance to stop them; I sincerely hope they will succeed, not succumb.

Monday in America

If more government is the answer, as liberals argue, then the 50% more of it that we added over the past decade would have proved their theory beyond a shadow of a doubt and I would be a raving socialist now. It did not, and I am not.

In fiscal year 2000, it cost us $3.2 trillion to run the government at all levels – local, state, and federal. In 2010, our government cost us $6.4 trillion - double. And not all due to undeclared wars and federal bailouts; state and local government doubled too, from $1.7 trillion to $3.4 trillion.

And how did we pay for all that additional government spending we added over the past decade? We borrowed it; the gross public debt - local, state, and federal – increased from $7.1 trillion to $16.7 trillion during the decade just past.

Democrats blame it all on Bush; Republicans put it all on Obama. It's like blaming the hangover on the last two drinks of a 100 year binger that started at Teddy Roosevelt's dorm room. National and local, Red states and Blue states, big cities and tiny villages – in fiscal terms, they have all been partying like it was 1999 since…1899.

It's 2011 now, and the lost decade is over. It's Monday in America, and with heads a-throbbing, we are staring at our staggering bar tab with disbelief.

After adjusting for inflation and the increase in population, the spending binge of the past decade amounts to more than a 50% increase in the size and cost of government. In real inflation-adjusted terms, we have added *half again* as much of the stuff as we had just ten years ago.

Did we ask for 50% more government in 2000? And does anyone feel 50% better governed now that we have 50% more of it? Do we have anything to show for our 50% increase in government other than that additional $9.6 trillion of new debt? Are we 50% happier?

Do we have 50% more roads, bridges, schools, airports, VA hospitals, fire stations, libraries, police precincts, national parks, ports, or postal deliveries? Did we add 25 more states, or maybe annex Canada? Is our response to natural disasters 50% faster? Are our children 50% better educated, our factories 50% more productive?

Did that increase of 50% in government bring about a 50% decrease in poverty, illiteracy, crime, disease, unemployment, drug abuse, domestic violence, teen pregnancy, high school dropout rates, pollution, gang violence, energy dependence, trade imbalances, workplace injuries, infant mortality, or fraud? Are we 50% safer, 50% more free and 50% more prosperous?

No, we are less safe, less free, and less prosperous – that is what we bought for 50% more government.

Just as Friedman, Hayek, Mises, Rand, Rothbard, Hazlitt, Paul and the framers of the Constitution told us. The other Friedman, Krugman, Keynes, Galbraith, Reich, Obama and all three Roosevelts promised we would be better off – they were wrong. Our only consolation is that we didn't go in for 75% or 100%.

Democrats are still chirping and clucking about insufficient resources as if the 50% increase never happened. Their talking points haven't changed since I first heard the pitch more than 40 years ago. Here's the deal, Dems: you got the money, you spent it, it didn't do jack squat, now give it up.

And Republicans prattle on as if it were a management problem they had nothing to do with, curable with better budgeting, an updated policy manual, and a dress code sure to improve productivity of the firm. With each new dose of GOP backtracking accountant-speak I am reminded why I left it years ago; I don't know how Ron Paul hangs in there. The new Congress has pledged to cut its office spending by 10%; a nice gesture, but the proportional equivalent of plucking a hair from a leg needing amputation.

Don't expect the government to shrink itself. The hysteria and hyperbole of government unions over the most modest of proposed reductions in the rate of increased spending tell us that reform must be done to them, not through them. When you bloat yourself up from 200 to 300 pounds and then threaten violence over cutting out one Twinkie a week, you are in need of some seriously tough love.

Our lost decade has shown us once again that Liberty, not government, is the path to peace and prosperity. Government spending is the true measure of liberty denied; and liberty's victories going forward will be tallied by dollars cut, not by promises made.

There is no intelligent argument to be made against cutting back on government; it will either be pared back or it will dissolve itself in certain default and the anarchy that will follow. A civil debate can, and should, center on how to save it; how much of it to eliminate and where. Those who refuse to participate opt for irrelevance and we should pay no heed to their protestations – you can't bring your stash to rehab.

The liberty movement that swept across the nation does not owe an allegiance to any party, party leader, or special interest. We are inspired by principle, led by conscience, and loyal only to ideas. We sent a new generation of representatives to Washington D.C. and statehouses, county seats, and town halls across the nation with a single purpose – to shrink government. We will judge them on how much they have accomplished by the next election in 2012.

Hope springs eternal, and everything that was done can be undone. It's Monday in America; the party's over, and it's time to go back to work.

Toxic

Five people were killed in Tucson Satuday; can you name them? John Roll, Gabe Zimmerman, Dorwin Stoddard, Dorothy Murray, Phyllis Sheck, Christine Greene. May God comfort their families, and may the rest of us have the human decency to leave our politics out of their grief.

The oldest was 79, the youngest only 9 – one pastor, one judge, one Congressional staffer, two in their twilight years and one whose life was just dawning. I suspect that the five life stories are fascinating, and the sixth would surely have been. 14 others were wounded, but we know the condition of only one – Congresswoman Giffords, on whose behalf the nation's prayers were offered and apparently answered. 48 hours after the senseless shooting in Arizona, we know very little about these 19 other victims, and only sketchy information about the man who struck them down.

But we know exactly what tens of thousands of politicos and bloggers think of the tea party, Sarah Palin, talk radio, communism, atheists, right and left wing rhetoric, guns, free speech, Republicans, Democrats, conservatives, libertarians, conspiracy theorists, the need for new prohibitions galore, and the precise motivation of a mentally disturbed person they have never met.

Their need to seize center-stage and co-opt a horrific personal tragedy to advance their own careers and ideologies is what is toxic in this country, not the phrases or symbols by which ideas are conveyed to the 310 million Americans who did *not* shoot anyone on Saturday. It took less than an hour for the mindless chattering class to chatter mindlessly.

The narcissism and callousness it takes to climb on top of 15 injured bodies to reach the microphone first is sickening - *that* is the toxicity that afflicts our nation, not the choice of phrases or symbols used to communicate with 310 million Americans who did *not* kill anyone on Saturday.

A senseless act, by definition, can not be understood in rational cause-and-effect terms. Only one person knows what deviant impulse led him to slaughter numbers of people, and the rest of us are recklessly projecting our own fears into his head. We may never know how that brain was molded over 22 years to become capable of such inhumanity; it most certainly did not get that way from one map on one web page, or anything that any of the victims may of may not have done to provoke the violence that was visited upon them. 19 of 20 were not public figures.

A shameless act, by definition, is one in which a lack of shame is displayed. Stepping on the grief of 20 families and the sympathies of a nation to draw the spotlight back onto partisan sparring is as shameless as I can imagine. It does nothing to bring comfort to the families; it only deepens the stress they must certainly be coping with, and injects the very toxicity it purports to decry.

These are days to respect the privacy and loss of the families, and to withhold opinions until they can be informed by facts and evidence. My condolences to the victims and their families, including the family of the man accused of the crime – they must be devastated, too. May God comfort them all in their time of greatest need.

Delusional

When my libertarian friends railed against the FCC's seizing authority over the internet right before Christmas, I honestly didn't get what all of the fuss was about. In the aftermath of the tragedy in Tucson, I get it. I *really* get it.

Imagine if Saturday's shooting would have occurred in internet-less world. The Sheriff would have linked the shooter to the Tea Party, and the mainstream media would run with it, embellishing the narrative to include Sarah Palin, talk radio, Arizona's immigration law, racism, and efforts to repeal the health care mandate and all the other crazy stuff that got thrown on the pile last Saturday in the world series of bullshit.

CBS, NBC, ABC, CNN, MSNBC, New York Times, Washington Post, L.A. Times, AP, Reuters – the media would report the Palin causal connection as fact, while the opinion pages would describe the tea parties as Klan rallies held in ammo dumps. Columnists and Congressmen would demand new prohibitions on guns, speech, association, and privacy, and legislatures would eagerly comply with hurried legislation in response to the clear and present danger posed by a "vast right-wing conspiracy" whose 20 Arizona victims are just the tip of the coming iceberg.

It is now quite clear that the Tucson narrative fabricated by the left was entirely wrong; ideology played no part in this tragic shooting whatsoever. Rather, an individual who was mentally ill set out to avenge a perceived personal slight when he tried to assassinate a Congresswoman for not adequately answering his previously asked question about grammar and word meanings.

But why do we know that? How did we come too learn the truth that it was a psychotic obsession with the meaning of words, and not our "toxic tone" in political debate that caused 20 people to be shot? The internet, that's how we know; that is the *only* reason we know. The same internet that the Government will soon censor, license, regulate, and monitor your usage of – the FCC's internet.

We did not learn the truth of Tucson from major news outlets, editorial writers, civic leaders, elected officials, law enforcement,

President, or Secretary of State, all of whom either parroted the lie or only begrudgingly acknowledged facts that others had discovered and tweeted, shared, reposted, and liked.

No, we learned the truth of Tucson from Youtube, MySpace, Facebook, Twitter, texting, and from thousands of bloggers who exposed the tea-party-did-it narrative as a vindictive partisan fraud within hours of its transparently coordinated launch.

Unfazed, MSM outlets continued to promote the big lie for days later, easily traversing the declining ethical half-lives that separate speculation from denial from deception from propaganda from delusion. As of this writing, they remain in a delusional state – trapped in a fantasy world of their own making where millions of tea-bots lurk locked-and-loaded and waiting for the fillings in their molars to vibrate with the low frequency signal from Palin and Beck to open fire.

Do you realize how close we came to our own American Kristallnacht? If the FCC had already developed its capability to block content – as it aims to do - which of the two Tucson narratives do you think would be suppressed in the name of "net neutrality": the statist party line wherein Sarah Palin and the tea party caused a massacre, or the alternative where a drug abusing mentally ill loner tried to kill a Congresswoman over an inadequate answer to his concern about grammar? When the bandwidth is prioritized by FCC, will you read about Tucson at Dr. Tim's Moment of Clarity or Paul Krugman's Daily Dose of Donkey Dung?

We would never know he was an atheist, a lunatic, a loner, a left-inspired anarchist drop-out with a history of violent threats and unstable impulses. We would know only what the government propagandist wants us to know – tea party did it. They would photoshop a Gadsden Flag hat on that bald head in his mug shot. It would be a blatant lie, a slander of the most despicable sort, a reckless smear whose sole purpose is to create the illusion of crisis requisite to convince the American people to cede more of our liberty to a government whose appetite for control is insatiable.

This is not paranoid speculation; we have just witnessed the new depths to which the left will sink to achieve their aims. For days now, we have read for ourselves the statist narrative that would have gone uncontroverted but for a free and unregulated internet. It is one thing for members of the media to jump to a wrong conclusion in a panic; such indiscretions are forgivable in the age of instant news and analysis.

But it is quite another to participate in a sustained coordinated campaign to distort, suppress, and misrepresent the truth. Not just some, but all of the major news outlets participated in the Tucson "toxic tone" conspiracy. None of them – not one – has apologized for the bile and invective they cast about and the character assassinations they unleashed without a scintilla of evidence to justify their charges.

It is because they have no remorse, no shame, no integrity. That is why they are broke and failing, no other reason.

They are not sorry for what they have done, and they will not be, because they believe their ends justify *any* means. They do not see that they have done wrong; only that it did not work; thwarted again by the internet and the millions of freethinkers who use it. These are the kind of people who go to work at FCC when their papers close down; regulating that internet that ruined their cushy lives to insure it fits the correct statist notion of "neutrality".

Now that we know what that term will mean shortly, Jerod Louchner's bizarre question to Congresswoman Giffords is positively chilling: "what is government if words have no meaning?" And here, my friends, is the adequate answer to his question: it is force - raw, brute, pure force. Fight back.

Campaign Finance Reform

Here is a proposal to bring transparency and ethics to the political process: repeal every single campaign finance reform law at every level, and force candidates to pay for their own campaigns.

Campaign finance laws are worse than nothing. Their main purpose is to provide an illusion of transparency by forcing donor A to fund candidate B through an elaborate lattice of fund transfers who have one purpose: to disguise the source of funds. It is licensed and regulated money laundering.

My union takes a dollar from me, then contributes it to the coalition of concerned-something-or-another, who pays $10,000 to sponsor a $5,000 booth at rally organized by Americans-for-whatever, which is a fundraising event whose proceeds are loaned to the national-wholesomeness-coalition, who commissions a study by the what's-the-answer-you-want Institute, to conduct "research" that will be plastered on a billboard paid for by citizens-against-douchebags that says "Call the other guy and tell him to quit eating our children". And when you call the number it is a robo-message paid for another committee set up to pour even more money into a campaign.

Or how about this, instead: I could give my guy a dollar. It's my dollar, it's his campaign.

Someone described campaign finance laws as planting trees on a hillside to prevent the rainwater from reaching the bottom - the water will always find its way around them. And building on the metaphor, most of the money in politics goes to watering the trees, so it takes massively more money than it used to. That's why millionaires beg billionaires for money to get elected.

There are a lot of mouths to feed shuffling all those dollars in and out of sight, and a high proportion of them have been capped and whitened professionally; the political class does not sweat the votes on minimum wage.

Do you know the difference between a 501(c)(3), a 501(c)(4), a 527, a PAC, a 501(c)(5), and a 501(c)(6) corporation? I hope not, and why should you? These are the different types of corporations that are exempt from paying taxes (isn't that convenient) because their revenues and profits are derived from political activities, not the exchange of goods and services. They are the six irrigation channels to route the water around the trees to the bottom of the hill.

Imagine if there was Bill Gates, Microsoft, Microsoft institute, Microsoft coalition, accountants for Microsoft, Microsoft network, Microsoft PAC, and Microsoft foundation - each of them a different corporate form (501, 527, PAC) with different rules and limits for donations, disbursements, and activities, some unlimited.

Campaign finance reform laws cap the contribution Bill Gates can make to a candidate as an individual, but do you have any doubt whatsoever that he could get as much money as he pleased into the hands of the candidate's campaign though his company and the six different channels that he controls?

Many of these supposedly firewalled organizations share employees, offices, and board members; many pay each other as consultants, provide services to each other for fees, and finance each other's operations with direct loans.

It's a corrupted mess that will not be fixed by more "restrictions" aimed at shutting down the other party's ability to raise and spend.

Regulated speech is not free speech, no matter who well-intentioned the regulation. Campaign finance laws just put more impediments for the little guys to get into the game. Scrap 'em.

Voter ID

Wisconsin's Republicans want to require a state-issued photo ID to vote in order to stop rampant voter fraud. Democrats oppose the measure, claiming that tens of thousands of voters would be disenfranchised – all Democrats, of course. Both positions are overblown, and neither can claim to be driven by noble principle with a straight face.

When all the partisan spinning, posing, and posturing are done, here's the deal: Republicans don't want elections decided by Mexicans, and Democrats don't want *any* restriction on their ability to fabricate vote counts. There's your moment of clarity.

If either party was truly interested in expanding voter empowerment, they would drop the rules put in place to stifle independent candidates and third parties.

Republicans are more than a little paranoid on this whole Mexican thing; millions of Mexican nationals are not pouring across the border hoping to work their way up to Wisconsin in time to vote against Paul Ryan in the next primary; they want jobs in Arizona and Texas. And felons and FIBS are not the reason that Gwen Moore and Tammy Baldwin have lifetime tenure in Congress; we could require a DNA match and carbon dating at the polls and it would not change the margins of victory that gerrymandering has engineered for them.

Democrats are even more disingenuous; the No-Chad-Left-Behind crowd is having kittens over voter ID while it is hell-bent on disenfranchising every single worker in the country by eliminating secret ballot union elections. Is there really an oppressed "community" who do not drive, fly, work, buy cigarettes, cash checks, fish, hunt, buy liquor, use credit cards, rent apartments, take out loans, get married, go to the library, or request a public record – all of which require a State-issued photo ID – but do vote religiously? Hard to cram all that on a T-shirt and still have room for a rainbow.

Libertarians can come at the voter ID issue from either direction, but is frankly hard to get all indignant about something we do willingly to get our hockey tickets at the Will-Call box. On one hand, we reflexively oppose any form of "human license" required by the capital "S" State; on the other hand, we revere the Constitution and take the rights and responsibilities of citizenship quite seriously. The Supreme Court ruled decisively in 2008 that state voter ID laws are constitutional (national REAL ID is a whole different subject), so it really comes down to a pragmatic question: how much additional hassle should we impose to discourage and prevent vote tampering?

Here's what I think: in a Constitutional democracy, voting is sacrosanct. The United States of America was founded on the principle of self-sovereignty, where the authority to act is delegated to government from fully empowered citizens, not the other way around. Choosing the people who will hold temporary stewardship of those delegated powers is the most solemn obligation we have as citizens of our nation. It is not unreasonable to insist that only eligible citizens participate in our only civic sacrament.

Surely the danger posed to society from vote tampering is far greater than that posed by an underage puff on a Camel. Acts of voter fraud are certain to occur in each election cycle, while acts of terrorism are ridiculously improbable; and yet the government makes me show it a state-issued photo ID, a travel voucher, and my unit before I can fly on an airplane that does not belong to them.

Voter ID is not an undue hardship and the only class of people who will be disenfranchised when it is enacted is vote-riggers. They will have to move back to Illinois, and we will take the businesses they are taxing out of their state. Good trade.

A Sane Foreign Policy

For anyone still searching for their last straw, I would highly recommend the sight of the Communist Chinese flag perched above the U.S. flag during President Hu's recent state visit here. There's your moment of clarity.

But don't blame China for America's rapidly declining stature in the world – all they did was open the playbook from the ascendency of America in the 19th century, while we turned our back on everything that made us great. A rational foreign policy has three parts: 1) we will buy your stuff, 2) we will sell you our stuff, and 3) if you attack us we will obliterate you. There is no part 4. China gets that; we don't.

What is the blueprint for prosperity that the Chinese have followed? Free trade, sound money, rejection of socialism, private property, tax cuts, a rigorous educational system, a culture that celebrates individual achievement, non-interventionist foreign policy, high savings rates and low debt, choice and competition, and de-regulation of the private sector. Where did they get such ridiculously outdated and radical ideas? Do they read the Mises blog and watch Ron Paul clips on YouTube?

In one generation China has turned from a dirt-poor, dogmatic Communist slave-pen to an economic powerhouse that is the envy of the world, at least the part of the world that isn't living in socialist denial. In that same generation, we have squandered the liberty and prosperity that it took 150 years for our ancestors to secure for us.

In recent weeks, I have visited Shanghai and Detroit. I did not visit Shanghai in 1970, but I would venture to say that the thrill of victory and the agony of defeat have switched host cities in the past four decades. They are making millionaires while we are making excuses. And that's about all we make in this country anymore, having run off our industrialists to more hospitable nations eager to own the prosperity that capitalism – and only capitalism – reliably delivers.

The Chinese workers, students, and officials I talked with on my visit to Shanghai are not sweat-shop pack mules; they are proud of their independence from the state and downright giddy at the levels of prosperity they enjoy now under capitalism. They revere America for the unbridled liberty they imagine we still enjoy. They think George Washington, Abraham Lincoln, Ronald Reagan and Barack Obama are mold-stamped guardians of liberty; I did not have the heart to burst their bubble.

We should be encouraged by China's dramatic rise. If China can go from dirt-poor, dogmatic blood-red Communist slave-pen to capitalist rave-party in just one generation, imagine where the United States could be in a generation if we return to the principles that made this country – and China, and Hong Kong, and Singapore, South Korea, and Taiwan, for that matter – great.

I recall hearing a lecture 20 years ago where a foreign policy expert guaranteed that China could never become a world economic power because of its isolationist, non-interventionist, and non-engagement stance. As it turns out, non-entanglement was a brilliant strategy, just as Thomas Jefferson and boys told us. Hu knew, but President Obama is even more clueless than President Bush, who might have had a few clues. That's why one elevator is going down, while the other is going up.

Neo-cons insist that America be the world's policeman, while liberals insist America be its social worker. Libertarians are happy to be its tourists.

Got something to see or buy? We'll be there. Want to see Wisconsin Dells? C'mon over and buy some fudge while you are here. Republicans and Democrats both have an obsession with dense government-to-government trade agreements even though governments do not trade, and no one who actually does trade ever bothers to read what trade bureaucrats write to justify their irrelevant jobs.

Bringing sanity to our foreign policy is ridiculously simple, and a lot less expensive than ObamaCare. First, build 500 nuclear power plants ($1 billion each when you drop the useless paperwork and Luddite lawsuits) and we have all the grid energy we need without emitting a gram of carbon, sulfur, or nitrates. That leaves all of our coal for gasification to run our big vehicles and industrial machinery – we have 500 years of the stuff since we don't need it for electricity.

CAPITALISTA!

And once we have energy independence, we don't need Middle East oil, so we don't need the Middle East, so we don't need Middle East wars, so we don't need the UN to provide cover for our meddling there, and when we quit funding the UN all the European socialists and African dictators will have to go back home and nag us via e-mail where we can just spam-trap 'em and delete and save the cost of all those Waldorf salads at conferences we should walk out on anyway.

Still with me? Ditto IMF, World Bank, WTO, WHO; sell tickets for all I care, but no more voodoo funding for world-government freaks by taxing unemployment benefits here.

China is trading with Taiwan, South Korea, and Japan now, so we don't need to maintain our military garrisons in Asia, and we just disentangled Europe and the Middle East in the last paragraph. As soon as we ignore the world's most petulant nation-child – North Korea - he will quit pitching fits, suck his thumb, and go take a nap. If he doesn't? Let China deal with it, it's their neighborhood.

Since we're not the world's super-nanny anymore, we don't need a military big enough fight all 6.6 billion foreigners at once. And we can quit bribing countries to pretend like they agree with us – that is, eliminate foreign aid – now that we have no more circus-show votes on meaningless UN resolutions.

I'm not sure if all of that would eliminate the deficit, but it would put a pretty good dent in it. But the economic boom it would trigger would put us back on the express elevator to the penthouse, assuming that leaders smart enough to enact a sane foreign policy would also apply sanity to economic, fiscal, and monetary policies.

And that is how we will bring democracy, free-market capitalism, and liberty to the world – not by shoving it down their throats, but by showing how well it works when we let it. We did that once, now China is pulling a shift, and we need to make it our turn again. One generation is all it takes; just like they told me in Shanghai.

Right To Work

The principle is not difficult to grasp: if you are the owner of you, then you have a right to work. If you do not have the right to work, then someone else owns you. If you oppose your right to work, but you don't know who else it is that owns you, may I suggest...me.

We'll call it the TimFL-CIO, and here is how it works: the government forces your employer to withhold dues from each pay check and send them to...me. That's right - you will pay *me* to take away *your* right to work.

I will decide what wage you will work for; it will be a lot less than mine. I will decide your benefit package; it will be a lot worse than mine. I will decide your pension; it won't be guaranteed like mine is. Sorry, no car for you, but I get a new one every year, even after I retire. No foreign-made Prius for this guy, no way; union-made Escalade, thank you very much – smoked glass, spinners, maybe a little neon under the chassis. Us union bosses have an image to maintain, and TimFL-CIO is swimming with the big fish, baby.

And I will decide which candidates you will support with the dues your employer confiscated for me. I will decide which legislation you will be for, and which you will be against. My position on everything is your position. I will pick the leadership of TimFL-CIO and you can rest assured it will be...me. I will go to the TimFL-CIO convention in Vegas, the leadership training in Miami, and host the Superbowl party in Dallas. First-class tickets, penthouse suites, limo, and "secretaries" - lots and lots of secretaries. Ok, my wife won't let me go for the secretaries, but it was in the job description, I swear.

When I order another bargaining unit to go on strike, I will double your dues to help me...er...them cope. If you have a grievance, question, or even a suggestion at you workplace, you bring it to me, and I will decide whether or not to bother with it. However I settle it; it's settled. When you break my union rules, I'll fine you, and if you think I'm wrong, you can appeal it to...me. Tell you what - I will screw you over for half of what the other guys charge in monthly dues, how's that? Think of me as the Walmart of WEACs, the Target of Teamster, the stingy man's SEIU. 50% off – you can't go wrong!

Now, if TimFL-CIO seems like a rotten deal to you, that's because it is...a rotten deal. And if you are dumb enough to think it magically becomes a good deal when we double the price and put "amalgamated" or "brotherhood" or "international" or "association" in the name of the racket, then you probably deserve to lose your job. It's not like your unions can save it for you anyway.

Unions lost 612,000 members in 2010, according to the Bureau of Labor Statistics – that's what happens when you choke the life out of your employer. Unions now represent only 6.9% of the private sector workforce, the lowest proportion since the 1930's. It should come as no surprise that 93.1% of people who work think it is a bad idea to pay someone to take away their right to work. What is remarkable is that nearly 7% still don't get it.

When you add the fact that most union elections are won on slim margins, it puts the percentage of private sector workers who have chosen union representation of their own volition at around 4%, slightly more than the number who are gay, and far fewer than the number who are left-handed. That puts the Right-To-Work issue in its proper perspective, now, doesn't it?

Would we allow Right-To-Vote legislation to be blocked by the gay southpaw lobby in Madison? I think not. Would we permit free speech be restricted to support of the LGBT agenda written in cursive with a backward slant? Fat chance. Then why should we care what the unions think of RTW in Wisconsin? We are under no obligation to negotiate the dinner menu with cannibals. Our right to work is a civil right, not a policy preference.

There is only one reason unions have power and influence; they buy Democrat politicians with tons of cash - cash that was confiscated from worker pay checks in the only protection racket sanctioned by the State. Government employees are being held as human shields and money launderers so the unions can plunder state treasuries with impunity. Right-To-Work frees the hostages and shuts down the rackets. Pick your side.

All of the data tells us that low-tax, RTW states outperform high-tax, highly unionized states in terms of economic growth, job creation, unemployment, and fiscal health. Over the past decade, real personal income in Right-To-Work states has increased at *double* the rate of forced-union states. The unionists' claim that passing RTW impoverishes people is a flat-out lie. 22 states have enacted Right To Work protection and prospered; the other 28 states need to join them. A coalition of conservative and libertarian voters fired the Democrats in November and put the GOP in charge of fixing our hostile business climate. So fix it, Party of Preibus.

The percentage of unionized workers in the private sector has shrunk by nearly 70% in the past 40 years. One need look no further than Detroit, that monument to UAW political influence, to see why thinking people choose not to sacrifice a life of work for a slogan. Or the idle mines of Upper Michigan, or the empty steel mills of Pittsburgh, or the vacant shipyards of Baltimore and Philadelphia, or the whole state of California, whose unions have brought it so low that Mexico doesn't want it back any more.

This year, government workers are about to discover what permanently unemployed textile workers up and down the East Coast already know: the only people who prosper under the unions are the union bosses. *Norma Rae* was a movie; the reality show has a much different ending. As states and municipalities face the spectre of bankruptcy, jobs will be cut, pensions will be reduced, and the unions will have killed yet another goose that could have laid golden eggs for generations to come. Too bad we let them take our schools down with them in their Epic Fail.

American workers are not stupid; our politicians are. The Right To Work for the 96% of us who choose to work union-free is guaranteed by the Constitution, as is the Right To Organize that 4% of us have freely chosen. By imposing compulsory unionization, our government denies the civil rights of the former to reward the thugs who claim to represent the latter. Stacking the NLRB with extortionists does not make extortion right, it just makes it easier.

Democrats have totally sold out to dirty union money. The Libertarian Party unequivocally defends the individual Right To

Work in our principled party platform. Where are the Republicans? 96% of American workers would like to know.

One In A Roe

While the President made decent jokes about salmon and TSA pat-downs in his State-Of-Delusion speech Tuesday night, the real howler came out on Monday, when he released the following statement on abortion:

"Today marks the 38th anniversary of Roe v. Wade, the Supreme Court decision that protects women's health and reproductive freedom, and affirms a fundamental principle: that government should not intrude on private family matters. I am committed to protecting this constitutional right."

Committed to not intrude on private family matters? There's one in a Roe.

Now, don't think this a post about abortion; that is a serious subject and it is getting harder and harder to take anything the President says seriously anymore.

No, this column is about the hypocrisy of inventing a constitutional right for that one solitary purpose, while totally disregarding the explicit constitutional protections that govern all other matters; the absurdity of being pro-choice on only one thing, and choosing the termination of life as your one thing.

Did the President really say with a straight face that he is committed to the fundamental principle of keeping the government from intruding on private family matters? How about invoking that fundamental principle on such private family matters as what we choose to eat, drink, smoke, drive, buy, sell, own, shoot, carry, pray, earn, save, drive, ride, wear, teach, grow, insure, say, pay, contribute, hunt, fish, advertise, marry, listen to, access on-line, heat our homes with, travel to, or pass to our heirs?

Abortion is a decision that the majority of women and all of us men will never have to face; and those women who do will visit it only once or twice in their lifetimes. But in all other areas of our lives, unwelcome and unconstitutional government intrusions are a daily occurrence and growing more frequent each time one of Obama's Czars picks up a pen.

His "commitment" to constitutional rights must have a provision for some of those infamous Obama waivers, because I cannot think of any three Presidents *combined* who have sought to intrude on private family matters as much as this guy has. And when he runs out of us people to lord over, he moves on to the critters - according to his State of the Union speech, we now have three agencies "in charge of the salmon". In charge? If I was a salmon, I would be already be organizing a tea party and fitting Sarah Palin with scuba gear out of spite.

Pro-lifers believe that life begins at conception. Pro-choicers believe life begins at the point of viability independent of the mother. Statists believe that life begins at the moment they can register one more living thing to regulate the crap out of and it ends when there is nothing left to tax.

Mr. Obama's support for abortion rights is not surprising; the unborn child is not yet available to the State anyway so it is of no use to those of his ideological bent. His government can afford to wait for the next one; it claims ownership of the CO_2 in the newborn's first wail, and it is all downhill from there. To demand that an individual be protected from government interference for his/her first nine months of life, and then be subjugated for the hundreds of months that will follow is the kind of irrational thinking that appeals to people who prefer to do very little of it – people who require two sittings to take in "hope and change".

There was nothing newsworthy in the President's SOTU speech. But I wish he wouldn't have called for science to receive as much attention as the Super Bowl, because now Brett Favre will probably try to come out of retirement and play quarterback for that Science Fairs team Mr. Obama referred to, if his agent can find out what city they play in. Or maybe not. Or maybe. Depends. Kinda.

The House repealed ObamaCare last week, and in 2012 the rest of us will get our turn to repeal its namesake at the polls. In the meantime, we will have to endure a few more rambling repetitions of the liberal mantra – trains, taxes, and tenure. And a few more moments of bald-faced hooey like "the government should not intrude on private family matters", which will remind me to thank my son for teaching me what ROTFLMAO means in text-speak.

CAPITALISTA!

How Many Architects?

The statists' argument that government intervention is necessary to correct market failures is easily defeated by asking just this one simple question: how many more architects do we need?

The belief that government must intervene to correct market failures rests on the assumption that government always knows the "right" answer; how else could it determine when the market has arrived at the wrong one? The absurdity of that notion is quite evident when we think about how the central planners would go about determining the "right" number of additional architects we need.

To figure out how many more architects we need, they would first need know how many we have, and how old they are, and when each one will retire, get too sick to work, move, or die. Next, they would need to know how many projects will be proposed and then undertaken in every city in the nation, along with how many hours each will take to be designed. To know that, they would need to know the future building plans and financial condition of every company, non-profit, and person in this nation, along with their style preferences and schedules for starting and completing their projects.

Not to mention the availability and cost of credit to finance these projects, which means they must know what the Federal Reserve and thousands of banks will do with interest rates in response to general economic conditions. This, naturally, means they would need to know what the general economic conditions are going to be, and since the economy is global, that means they would have to know basically everything there is to know about everything everywhere. No doubt that President we-do-big-things Obama would call this massive and futile undertaking an investment in our future.

Since it takes about ten years to educate and field an experienced architect, they would need to know everything about everything for the next ten years of economic activity world-wide. The statist's first instinct would be to overcome this dilemma by requiring everyone in the world apply for daily living permits that must be approved ten years in advance, and load all of the economic decisions into a massive computer model.

Given the government's inability to forecast next weeks' new unemployment claims, the chances of projecting trillions of variable data points ten years into the future and coming up anywhere remotely close to the right number of architects needed are exactly...zero. And the government would not just get it hopelessly wrong; it would spend hundreds of billions of dollars to get it hopelessly wrong. And we would all spend our entire days filling out the forms it would need to collect all the data required to be hopelessly wrong in the digital age.

Yet markets accomplish this feat with ease. Game, set, match.

Have you ever needed an architect and had to wait ten years for the next one to become available? Are there millions of surplus architects hanging out at Home Depot or perched at traffic islands holding homemade signs that say "will enhance dimensional context for food"? No, you haven't, and no, there aren't. Free markets do not produce chronic surpluses and shortages; it takes government intervention to produce such distortions.

Markets supply the right numbers of architects to the right numbers of firms without anyone forcing anyone else to do anything. How? The same way markets supply the right numbers of thousands of professions to millions of employers every day - by simply allowing people to make self-interested choices of their own volition. The invisible hand of capitalist free markets performs this and every other economic task far better, far faster, and far cheaper than the heavy hand of coercive government.

For nearly a century, government has taken upon itself the authority to intervene and impose its we-know-better judgment on wages, benefits, working conditions, credentials, union membership, and licensure. Along the way it has promulgated innumerable industry-specific mandates and restrictions, and outlawed some professions altogether. The more it tries to "help", the worse of a mess it makes.

With the passage of ObamaCare, the State greatly raised the stakes for inadvisable market intervention; it will soon impose its own judgments over how many doctors and nurses will practice and how much they will get reimbursed for their services. The rationale for this unprecedented intervention of central planning is to "keep the private sector honest", and to correct the "failures of the market".

But before we go ahead and turn over nearly one fifth of our economy – and the labor markets for those professions who will make our most critical life and death decisions - to Mr. Obama's beloved central planners, I think it is prudent to ask him just one question, if I may.

Mr. President - how many more architects to we need?

Trail of Lies

A second federal court has now ruled that ObamaCare is unconstitutional, and the Democrats' predictable response is to ignore the ruling. And to misrepresent two earlier procedural dismissals as constitutional endorsements in order to claim a 2-2 tie in court cases.

Only two cases were allowed to move forward to a final judgment; in both cases, the court found the Patient Protection and Affordable Care Act to be unconstitutional. The score is 2-0 with 2 abstentions. Until it is overturned or stayed on appeal, Judge Vinson's ruling makes ObamaCare as unenforceable as a slave contract.

You would not get that impression from the herd media. It should not surprise anyone that Obama's cheer squad would be less than forthright about the courts voiding their guy's landmark legislative achievement. They have been dishonest bout health care reform from the jump – it has been a long trail of lies.

There never were 45 million Americans without health care; that was a lie. The law requires hospitals and physicians to treat all patients in need of care.

There never were 45 million Americans uninsured; that was a lie. That number was proven to be 4-5 times overstated. And many who were actually denied insurance coverage were eligible for state assistance.

The nation was never crying out for socialized medicine. Polls have shown Americans opposed to the President's Health Care Reform Bill consistently by nearly 3:1. It got worse once we found out what was in it.

Candidate Obama promised you would not be forced to buy insurance; that was a lie. The mandate to purchase insurance is the cornerstone of the whole plan.

The President promised there would be no tax increases; that was a lie. The Bill contains dozens of tax increases.

The President promised you could keep your current employer plan; that was a lie. The Bill forced every single plan to be changed within the first year of its passage.

The Bill was supposed to bend the cost curve; that was a lie. Within weeks of passage, premiums soared.

The Bill was going to reduce the deficit; that was a lie. CBO used 10 years of tax increases and 5 years of benefit costs and omitted the Medicare Fix to show a "savings".

The Bill was not available to the public before voting; that was a lie. The process was not transparent; that was a lie. Reconciliation is not a common parliamentary procedure; that was a lie. They were prepared to "deem" it passed if necessary; that was a lie. The bi-partisan summit was a lie. The Executive Order which bought pro-life Democrat Bart Stupak's vote has already been abrogated.

The whole thing was a fraud. Only a guy from Chicago would think he could get away with it, and only a sell-out would cash a journalists' pay check to help him.

The big insurance companies, hospital chains, and pharmaceutical giants got 32 million new customers handed to them as payback for their campaign contributions. The little guys got screwed, the unions got waivers, and you got stuck with the tab. That's the truth about ObamaCare.

The free lunch crowd got hoodwinked into thinking a whole new buffet would kick in at 2014, two years too late to vote against the guy who sold them the snake oil. Poor bastards still think they got free health care coming any day now.

President Obama wasted half of his term and two years of the nation's economic non-recovery to get this steaming pile of a bill passed, and now it has been blown to smithereens by a Federal Judge who simply did what the Democrats in the legislature and the White House failed to do - apply the Constitution.

Any eighth-grader would know that PPACA is unconstitutional - it takes eight years of Ivy League education not to care.

CAPITALISTA!

Health Care Reform is President Obama's own Iraq – an ideological blunder of epic proportions - and those 45 million phantom uninsured are his WMD.

The Democrats' own mission-accomplished moment has got to be Nancy Pelosi's ode to arrogance - "are you serious?" - which she spat in response to a question about the constitutional authorization for the Bill.

That one moment of unvarnished truth re-invigorated a Tea Party revolt that will not now go away; it brought on a thumping at the polls in November, a repeal of the bill in the House, and the introduction of measures to defund and defang in the Senate. And not one, but two federal court decisions that nullify the Bill.

Yes, Nancy, we are serious.

Rational Defense

Liberals expose themselves to ridicule when they measure compassion by government spending on social programs. Conservatives make the same mistake when they equate spending on national defense with national defense.

Conservatives and libertarians see eye-to-eye on many things, but we usually part company when it comes to National Defense. Defense is a subject I know a little bit about, with 35 years of experience in the industry and a doctoral dissertation on DoD procurement practices and their impact on small businesses.

Propose to cut defense spending and most conservatives will reflexively object, as if our nation's enemies are deterred by budgets rather than bullets, and appropriations instead of artillery. It is quite unlikely that Al Qaeda knows or cares what percentage of GDP we spend on Defense, and troublemakers closer to home, like Hugo Chavez, do not lose any sleep over the Divisions we have permanently garrisoned in South Korea, Japan, and Germany.

The rational argument can, and should, be made that decades of excessive spending on the defense of other nations has weakened, not strengthened, our own defenses. It is the American defense of Europe that permits them to spend their own resources on expanding their welfare states, promoting world government, and subsidizing exports that cost American jobs.

It is our mutual defense obligations in Asia that have set us on a collision course with North Korea, a puny nation that could not land a missile on our shores if we gave them the submarines to launch from. Our Korean peninsula entanglements allow China to ignore their lunatic next-door neighbor and focus on buying up U.S. assets while we do their dirty work of containment.

The still-hostile Middle East is home to 21 U.S. permanent military bases, not counting the wartime camps in Afghanistan and Iraq and the Navy's carrier battle groups permanently patrolling off the region's coasts. You won't hear me apologizing for Iran's belligerence and uncivilized posture towards the community of nations, but the paranoia of its leaders is not altogether unreasonable when you look at the map of U.S. troop deployments that surround them.

Spending and necessary spending are two different things. The United States Department of Defense boasts 1.1 million spectacular men and women in uniform and then it adds an astonishing 600,000 civilian employees, whose primary job is to buy bullets, beans, and band-aids for the troops. No CEO would survive a week if his factory had 1,100 people on the assembly line and 600 purchasing agents in cubes.

DoD is one of the most inefficient, bloated bureaucracies on the planet, and anyone who has served, worked, or contracted for it knows this to be true. Its mission is as much about defending its civil-service make-work jobs as it is defending our shores. Are those featherbedded jobs off limits to the budget busters, simply because the House of Glut has five sides? I think not.

From 1990 to 2000, the largest 100 Defense contractors were consolidated through mergers and acquisition down to just five firms – the original too-big-to-fail club. Prime contracts are rarely subjected to true competition; how could they be, when there is only one shipyard capable of building aircraft carriers, and it operates for all practical purposes as a public utility? While it is essential that the United States maintain an industrial base capable of supplying our own military, it is not essential that firms who supply the military are immunized from market forces by arcane procurement practices that make innovation impossible and best practice illegal.

Many libertarians exhibit a pacifists' aversion to all-things-military, but I am not one of them. While liberty is the natural state of being intended by our Creator, it is not the default setting for governments around the world. Liberty attracts powerful enemies from whom it must be constantly defended. Our Constitution provides for a stout defense; it requires Congress to maintain a Navy, to protect trade routes, to raise armies, to declare wars, to put down insurrections, and to secure U.S. territory against aggression.

But the Constitution does not authorize Congress to fund undeclared military interventions abroad, to establish permanent garrisons around the world, to prop up undemocratic foreign regimes through Foreign Military Sales, to engage in "nation building", to ignore the 4th amendment based on a color chart, or to enrich a handful of American pseudo-corporations who are totally dependent upon government spending for their existence.

When Congressman Ron Paul called it the warfare/welfare state, the derision conservatives heaped upon him for speaking the truth is shameful. Conservative candidates for office often must "prove" their toughness in terms of supporting a minimum percentage of GDP to be spent on Defense, usually in the 4-5% range.

This totally misses the point; Defense is not GDP insurance, or some derivative of death to be hedged statistically. If Bernanke cranks up GDP by a couple of phony trillions, it does not increase the threat to national security one iota; likewise if we would restate our economic condition honestly, threats would not disappear because the real value of our nation's output is lower than previously claimed.

Terrorism is real; the potential threat from China is real; the bad intentions of Iran and North Korea are real; piracy is real; and the insurrection at our southern border is real. Cyber-threats are real and more prevalent than most of us would care to believe if we knew the truth. We need a strong and vigorous national defense; our liberty is best preserved by the certain assurance that those foolish enough to attack us will be swiftly and utterly destroyed. Key word: *us.*

That assurance can be purchased for *less than half* of what we spend each year on so-called Defense. This is the awkward truth that must be confronted if Republicans are to be taken seriously as deficit hawks. Without eliminating the $375 billion annually that is squandered to defend other nations, fight undeclared wars, reward special interests, and provide lifetime jobs for cube jockeys who can't field-strip a weapon, it is simply not possible to eliminate the deficit. Without raising taxes.

Defending our own nation is one thing; defending a vague "stable world order" is something quite different. If nations like Bulgaria, Kyrgyzstan, Singapore, Portugal, Qatar, Philippines, Turkey, Kosovo, and Bahrain are deemed so vital to our strategic interest as to warrant permanently basing troops there, then the only limit on our expanding military footprint is fiscal insanity.

And fiscal insanity is right where we find ourselves – borrowing money from China to dole out in military aid to despots in countries whose names we cannot pronounce. Our enemy at the gate is not the Lebanese Navy; it is our crushing debt load.

Cutting Defense spending may drive a wedge between conservatives and strident neo-conservatives, but it will reunite classical conservatives with libertarians and independents to forge an unbeatable coalition of fiscally responsible voters that will easily win the day in 2012. But politics is not the reason to cut Defense spending; national defense is the reason to cut Defense spending.

Our nation will be better defended, our military will be returned to its noble purpose, and the service of all who ever put on the uniform and took the oath to uphold and defend the Constitution will be honored by cutting unnecessary and unconstitutional spending on Defense. And it will fuel the economic recovery that will restore liberty to the nation which claims it as its first principle.

The Solution

Overheard this morning on the D.C. Metro commute to Capitol Hill, "...and he just went mental - turned into some kind of giant tea-bagger, totally against the government now, not even interested in being part of the solution anymore".

Overheard in the Senate cafeteria later today, "...it's too late to get you an earmark this year, but there will be plenty of chances for plus-ups in the appropriations bills; we appreciate the fundraisers you put on last year".

Two eavesdropped snippets of two different conversations on an ordinary Tuesday in our nation's capital perfectly encapsulated the two things fundamentally wrong with our government - the fairy tale belief that it can solve every problem, and the ugly truth that its appropriations are for sale to the highest bidder.

Can you think of the last problem that government solved? Certainly not crime, drugs, education, poverty, energy, trade, inflation, disaster response, employment, health, divorce, rogue states, teenage pregnancy, avoidance of war, nutrition, terrorism, border security, pension solvency, or housing.

To be fair, the air and water were cleaned up in the 1970's, and that was a good thing. Defeating communism in the 1980's was another. But only two hits in four decades? It must suck to know you are less relevant than Cher.

My Tuesday in Washington was capped off with the late afternoon release of the final report that exonerated Toyota, the non-union automaker who was falsely accused of accelerator safety violations shortly after the government bought General Motors for the UAW. No apologies from anyone over there in "The Solution" for the billions of damage it inflicted on the company out of spite.

What does the Toyota case have to do with earmarks and the Tea Party? Ray La Hood, President Obama's Secretary of Transportation. A Republican former Congressman from Illinois (that explains it) and the guy who warned all Toyota owners to "leave their cars parked in the garage", La Hood scored a 0%

rating from the anti-earmark Club For Growth in 2007, and less than 50% lifetime rating from Citizens Against Government Waste. Republocrat; porkmeister; petty tyrant, point man for high-speed rail. Thousands of bright young Hill staffers hope to be just like him someday, and that in itself is a travesty worth fighting.

My solution for "The Solution"? This government can not be effectively reformed; it must be dismantled.

That is the message of the Tea Party, and the reason that lovers of failed government – like those two impressionables on the Metro - are right to fear the liberty movement. Not because we are violent or racist - watch the video of the liberal protestors at the Koch retreat if you want to see what that looks like - but because it is pure foolishness to keep funding failure.

A business does not continue to build products that do not work, doctors do not continue to prescribe medicines with harmful side effects, and nobody keeps giving bums money they spend on rot-gut, no matter how convincing the ask.

But a government program goes on forever, regardless of whether or not it ever solves the problem that justified its creation. In fact, the worse it makes the problem, the more money it gets, and the more staffers like the one in the cafeteria get to dole it out to donors and benefactors of the Parties.

Program by program, agency by agency, department by department, the foolishness must be called out and then ended. People who can't tell the difference between a solution and a failure will never be able to improve their own performance – we are kidding ourselves to think they will be persuaded to work smarter by having the Constitution read to them. They are not evil, they are inexperienced and ignorant. We all started out that way.

The best thing for them is to liberate them from their triplicate forms and endless meetings to go find work where solutions are rewarded and failure is punished – i.e. the private sector – so they learn the difference quickly and are able to reach their full economic potential.

I would like to meet that kid who "went mental" and turned his back on "The Solution" - it takes some guts to think for yourself at that age. I'm happy for him that he will not spend his life pimping appropriations and watching porn in his cube, counting the days until his pension kicks in.

He and others like him are the real solution to this nation's problems. Dependence on government is what has brought us low; independence from government is what will restore our greatness in the world. I'm glad that he chose independence.

In God We Trust

Anyone who still wants the phrase "In God We Trust" removed from our currency should consider the alternative, Fed Chairman Ben Bernanke.

This week, Chairman Bernanke testified at the House Budget Committee that the Fed's monetary policy had achieved their target GDP growth rate of 3.4% in the fourth quarter of 2010. He explained to us that 5% was too fast, and 2% was too slow, and that growth in the mid-3's was just right. Later, in a response to a question on unemployment, he calculated that with growth rates in the mid-3's it would take ten years to bring unemployment down to 5%.

Ten years! In the third year of a recession brought about in large measure by the Fed's own monetary policy mistakes, its Chairman told us to buck up and expect another *decade* of joblessness – best he can do, sorry. Maybe you prefer to trust the Fed, but I'm sticking with God, thank you very much.

The Federal Reserve is an extension of the Treasury Department on one hand, and an extension of a bank cartel that owns it on the other; that is a cozy little arrangement. Perhaps you trust bankers and bureaucrats, but once again, I'm going with God.

The Fed creates hundreds of billions from thin air, gives the monopoly money at essentially zero interest to its member banks, which turn right around seconds later and loan it to Treasury at almost 4% through the purchase of government bonds. That is how the government keeps expanding while real GDP growth and tax revenues decline. Clever, but I'll still take God.

Bernanke's "quantitative easing" gives almost 4 percentage points of risk-free profit, plus some hefty processing fees, to the banks for clicking a mouse a couple of times. Why would banks want to lend any of it to individuals and businesses and run the risk of non-payment to gain what – maybe a percent or two more? They trust Bernanke, reason enough for me to choose God right there.

People often assume that there is a single monolithic "business community" out there. This imaginary cadre of greedy capitalists are the favorite whipping boys (and they are all boys, don't you know, white boys to boot) of socialist politicians and class-envy pimps the world over. The truth is, those of us who create wealth don't much care for the bankers who hold it for us. We never did trust them - that's probably why they had to name-drop God's endorsement on their fiat money in the first place.

Bernanke's money-laundering scheme would be – and should be - shut down if Congress votes not to increase the debt ceiling in a few weeks. 70% of Americans want them to hold the line on borrowing just like we overwhelmingly opposed TARP, GM, Stimulus, Health Care Reform, and the drilling ban – so get ready to have your heart broken again. Ben has already threatened economic Armageddon if he doesn't get his credit limit raised, but I'm siding with the dude who can bring the real Armageddon.

In response to House Members questions about how to restore economic health, he blinked and coughed a lot. He did not differentiate between tax increases and spending cuts; he did not differentiate between spending and investing, he did not differentiate between saving and inflating the money supply. He did not seem very interested in the relationship between public policy choices and private economic behavior. It was not surprising, as those are economic questions, and he is a mathematician by trade. I know the man has a doctorate, but I'm still trusting God – with help from Ron Paul.

As luck would have it, Bernanke's blather was upstaged by EPA Administrator Lisa Jackson, who made him look like a bloody Mensa wizard when it comes to economic theory. Her outside-the-bun idea this week was to force companies "hording" $1.9 trillion of cash reserves to invest them in "green" technologies to create jobs. Yeah, that's exactly what we need, Lisa. Bernanke's in 2nd, behind…God.

The basic principle underpinning her proposal is "you have it and I want it", which is not really economics as much as looting 101. That made perfect sense to the delegates at a convention of labor unions and environmental activists where she hatched the idea, since the jobs created would be more EPA environmental activists who belong to the union. They gave her boxing gloves as an award for fighting against companies at the same time President Obama 2.0 was over at the U.S. Chamber of Commerce assuring them that we are all in this together. Yup, it's God.

The reason that corporations have accumulated $1.9 trillion in surpluses is that we don't listen to idiots like Ms. Jackson. There would not be $1.9 trillion on corporate balance sheets if companies invested their retained earnings into stupid projects that are not economically viable; and the last place on earth we would think to seek advice on economic viability is Washington, D.C.

The objective of any business is to build wealth – to earn more than they spend. It is not to assist partisan hacks advance their personal empire-building agendas. Not to belabor the point, but corporations (and 99% of them have less than 50 employees) accumulating wealth is the only reason there is *any* money to pay for Ms. Jackson and her precious monstrosity EPA, or Ben Bernanke and his beloved Fed, or the Congress which will almost certainly cave and raise the debt ceiling.

Corporations invest in projects that offer a return that is proportionate to their risk of loss. With President Obama and his crew at the helm, clearly America's CEO's have decided that in this economic environment the risk of loss is so nearly certain that $2 trillion has accumulated, waiting for economic conditions to become favorable – i.e. for the next election to usher in people who know what they are doing.

So until that day comes, I am trusting in God, just like my Federal Reserve Notes tell me to.

PART THREE: THE CIVIL WAR BEGINS IN WISCONSIN

February – April 2011

Walker, Wisconsin Ranger

Wisconsin Governor Walker put it to the state's unions this week: either a) state workers accept a modest benefit concession, or b) he cuts 22,500 government jobs and drops 200,000 kids from BadgerCare, the health care safety net for poor children.

As expected, the unionists rejected any talk of benefit reform outright, choosing instead to throw those kids under the bus along with their least senior brethren. Solidarity forever – or until we have to contribute something to our fat pensions, whichever comes first.

The reduced benefits which the Governor will impose will still leave state employees with far higher pay than their private sector counterparts and with much richer benefit packages. But to read the comments posted by union workers to articles announcing the Governors plan, you would think he ordered not just sub-minimum wage but also genital amputation for all state workers.

93% of private sector workers choose not to have union representation, and the paupers' cemeteries are not filled to overflowing with the broken bodies of penniless folks flogged to an early death. State workers are being asked to make modest contributions to health insurance and retirement plans, at levels that private sector workers started making 20 years ago. The louder they wail about it, the more it appears to the rest of us they have been clueless for most of that time.

The Governor wrote a polite and respectful letter to state employees explaining the urgency of the need for actions and the specifics of what he will do to insure the state will not go into default before the end of the fiscal year. It would be a good thing for the unionists to quit yelling long enough to read it, understand that no one is taking away their firstborns to the stewpots, and then contemplate what that default would mean to them.

They would all lose their jobs, their benefits, and their pensions - everything. If they do not accept benefit reforms, state workers will have Enron-ed themselves when they had the chance to avoid it. And that is the cliff over which their union leadership is pushing them; easy for him when his paycheck won't be affected and he makes more than the Governor.

Lost in all the hysteria over what is in truth a modest benefit reform was another provision in the budget repair plan that may end up being far more significant – Walker's plan would require state workers to re-certify their unions each year. This is a novel idea.

Libertarians respect every person's right to form and join a union, along with every person's equal right *not* to join a union. An outright ban on public unions, as some conservatives have called for, would deny one of these counterbalanced rights, and so we don't go there.

We advocate Right To Work laws that give each individual his/her choice regarding union membership. RTW is a plank in the Libertarian Party platform and we have joined with others to lead the push to have Worker's Choice legislation enacted in Wisconsin.

But annual recertification for public unions is a big step forward, and a pragmatic middle ground – it provides a mechanism for state employees to throw off the yoke of inept, corrupt, and harmful union representation. And it forces their unions to remain relevant, reasonable, and value-adding if they want to avoid extinction.

A union that does all the wonderful things that AFSCME claims to do for its members will have no trouble whatsoever being recertified year after year. I belong to about a dozen organizations that have annual renewals and none of them rely on the protection of the State; they just operate in such a way that I want to renew of my own volition. And when they don't (listening, NRA?), we part company. Until RTW is passed, the next best thing is annual certification renewal.

Governor Walker is a conservative Republican, and no one should be surprised that he is acting like one. There will be plenty of issues where he will not enjoy libertarian support, but we must stand with him on this one. His stance is courageous, his plan is reasonable, and the need for reform is urgent as we are months, not years, away from running out of funds and triggering default.

Forced unionization is antithetical to the principle of individual liberty. Public sector unions present double jeopardy, as they expand the scope and power of the state, further diminishing liberty as the inevitable consequence. Governor Walker is standing for liberty, and AFSCME stands opposed.

Pick your side.

Walker, Wisconsin Ranger – Part II

Last week, I supported Wisconsin Governor Scott Walker's plan to impose modest benefit concessions on all public workers to avoid laying off tens of thousands of them. I have changed my mind; he should get rid of as many of them as possible.

No, seriously - the fewer the better.

The public employees' protests over the past few days have convinced me that we do not need to compensate our public sector employees reasonably; we need to keep as many of them as possible as far away as possible from doing anything that is remotely important.

When the keynote speaker at a UWM rally on the importance of a union education sounds like a Valley Girl with Tourette's Syndrome, I don't want any of them teaching our kids – not at any price. For all I know, she has an IQ with a comma in it, but her 14-plus years of union indoctrination in government schools have made her dumber than a box of hair.

The only purpose of education is to prepare children to succeed as productive adult citizens. Dropping F-bombs and rambling in incoherent thumb-language does not make you productive; it makes you a worthless parasite that will not survive a day on your own.

To all of my friends who belong to public unions, I can only beg you to decertify before this gets any worse. Save yourselves while there is time. We don't hate bus drivers, or road crews, or policemen, or social workers, or teachers; but every time you have a rally, your leaders give us another reason to start. Pick anyone else and they will do better – here are a few tips to get started:

First of all, if you are going to make an appeal to our better nature, don't start by calling us mentally retarded. You don't get very far talking to the boss like that.

Second, don't expect much sympathy when you can't even turn out 1,000 to rally on your own day off, but then you bus in tens of thousands on a workday when you are on the clock. This does not impress us.

Third, making school kids leave class to carry your picket signs at the Capitol was so stupid even that Tourette's Valley Girl can't string together enough "effin's" to describe it.

The kids in China and India were too busy learning math today to carry signs for more teacher pay, and that is why they are kicking our asses. Either get that or get out.

Fourth, if you have a better idea – check that, ANY idea - of how to close Wisconsin's $3.3 billion budget deficit, then please, PLEASE, spell it out for us. If not, then shut the "eff" up, to borrow a phrase from UWM's YouTube Miss Congeniality.

I've been begging for two weeks to see your Plan B – I will print it here if you will send it to me. You guys are math teachers, economists, political science professors, and actuaries. The public sector is your field, not ours; you have had about a dozen years to see this day coming, so let's hear your plan to avoid default.

Here's the deal: a guy with about a month on the job put together a plan that fixes the state's budget gap. You guys don't like it, but with your millions of years of experience and tens of thousands of advanced university degrees you have no alternative to offer except to hold your breath and stomp your feet.

And you expect that will make us side with you? What kind of bubble do you live in where no plan beats a plan? Where name-calling beats a respectful explanation of position? Where you walk off some of the best-paying jobs in the state to complain about a benefit reform that leaves you twice as well-off as the people paying your compensation?

You work hard – we get that. Everybody works hard; checkmate. And you broke the cardinal rule when you took the protest to his private residence – we are all done listening to you now.

So far, state employees' unions have offered nothing but name-calling and threats, and Governor Walker is going to win this battle by default.

Not because his plan is brilliant, but because he has the only one out there. State workers have offered no credible alternative, and the reservoir of good will they once enjoyed was poisoned forever with that stupid stunt in the Capitol.

Those are our kids; the unions were very foolish to use them in that way. And now it is the taxpayers' turn to bargain collectively.

War On Sanity

Someone needs to tell conservatives it's ok to question the War on Drugs. Milton Friedman, Bill Buckley, Barry Goldwater, Pat Buchanan, Grover Norquist, and others of unquestionable conservative bona fides have all touched that stovetop and lived to tell.

If you want to see a conservative Republican act like a liberal Democrat - defending a feel-good program that is obscenely expensive and worse than ineffective - bring up the war on drugs. Not working? Spend more. Still not working? Spend even more? It violates the 4th, 9th, and 10th, amendments – are you serious?

Don't get me wrong. I do not advocate drug use and have seen the devastating effect that drugs can have on people first hand. This is not about drugs; it is about ineffective policy. For 30 years we have spent nearly a trillion dollars in the War on Drugs and have not moved the needle a nit on either usage or addiction rates. It is all side effect and no cure.

The Office of National Drug Policy estimates that Americans spend $65 billion on illegal drugs each year. Based on retail prices in countries where drug prohibition has been repealed, Americans are overpaying by $35 billion. If it were insurance or oil companies selling dope at predatory prices, President Obama would nationalize them. But high prices and outrageous profits are the consequence of our drug laws, so it's all good, for reasons that defy any logical explanation. And we are missing out on $7 billion in taxes on profits by forcing this industry underground.

We can then tack on another $44 billion each year for the War on Drugs – that's what Harvard says it costs, anyway. The first $30 billion bought the dope, the next $35 billion is the windfall profit, and the last $44 billion buys us gangs, violence, crime, overcrowded prisons, decimated inner cities, police corruption, ungovernable schools, and regular violations of our 4th amendment rights under the Constitution.

It's a bad bargain. Combined, that is $86 billion per year peed away each year, not counting the market price of the drugs themselves. Politicians who claim to be deficit hawks but can't even find $100 billion to cut from the federal budget might want to give this a serious look-see. But it is a lot more than money that is at stake.

In 2009, the number of drug arrests was 1,663,582. Nearly half of those (758,593) were for simple possession of marijuana. That is more than all of the arrests for all violent crimes combined that year - 581,785. Think about how much of law enforcement's resources are devoted to prosecuting non-violent drug offenses, and how many violent crimes go unsolved or pled down due to lack of resources. And think of how many lives are ruined with a felony conviction for holding a plant.

The National Drug Intelligence Center states that deaths due to illegal drug use number "in the thousands". $85 billion to fight a problem measured in thousands? Are you kidding me? Over 100,000 people died of prescription drug mistakes last year, so how much should we spend on the War on Pharmacists - $8.5 trillion?

Where in the Constitution does it grand authority for federal agents to confiscate property on the suspicion of a crime? Where does it empower police officers to conduct random vehicle searches? Where does it allow for border agents to set up road blocks 100 miles away from the border? Where does it require states to conform to federal sentencing mandates? Why are all the other Obama Czars such a constitutional problem for conservatives, but not the drug Czar?

If the choice was drugs or no drugs, I vote no drugs. But that is not the choice we get in the real world – our choice is a) drugs, or b) drugs, gangs, violence, crimes, overcrowded prisons, destruction of our inner cities, and 30,000 people slaughtered in Mexico in a real drug war that is spilling over our southern borders.

Republicans and Democrats both pick option b. Republicans heap ridicule on anyone in their party – Ron Paul, Gary Johnson – who dare to challenge the orthodoxy on drug policy. Democrats would too, but they can't even find anyone to heap ridicule upon. I can guarantee you that that it is not libertarians who buy $65 billion of illicit drugs – there aren't enough of us and we don't make that much.

The nation learned a lesson during Prohibition and we corrected our mistake. It is time to do the same with the other substances we have licensed for free to organized crime. Ending the war on alcohol did not turn us into a nation of drunkards, and ending the war on drugs will not turn us into a nation of stoners, either. If heroin were legal tomorrow, would you go shoot up after breakfast? Me neither.

And do you really want your children or grandchildren going to prison and living with the stigma of a felony record because they were unlucky enough to get caught doing something that a majority of Americans has done at least once? Would you rather your kids snort bath salts, or drink after shave, or huff spray paint? Is that our idea or protecting public health? I hope not.

Here's what will happen when we repeal our drug prohibitions: the gangs will wither and die, the cartel warfare in Mexico will cease, our prisons will be manageable, our police can focus on fighting real crimes, fathers will return to the inner city, and we will be $85 billion to the good.

And yes - people who want to get high will get high, and those who can't handle it will become addicted, same as it ever was. There is only one power who can save them from themselves, and He does not need our laws to work His miracles on this earth.

It will be ok.

Liberate Education

Over the past several days, the fur has been flying in Wisconsin over Governor Walker's plan to modify state workers' benefit contributions as part of his budget fix package. Unionists object strongly to his suspension of collective bargaining rights, and as a libertarian, I agree with them on that one point – up to a point.

But if you are going to make the argument that a state law cannot deny someone their right to bargain collectively, then you must also concede the other half of the constitutional right to association – which is the right to work free of union impairment. State workers, including our teachers, do not recognize this reciprocal right, and therefore, lose a lot of support that would otherwise flow their way.

Wisconsin teachers are missing a golden opportunity here to reform a public education system that has been severely degraded by forced unionization and the seizing of control away from local authorities to the State Department of Public Instruction. I can't seem to pry an alternative to the Governor's plan from my teacher friends, so here you go, teachers – let me give you a libertarian alternative to chew on.

First of all, decertify your state-wide union, WEAC, drop out of NEA, and then decide locally what type of collective representation, if any, you will choose for yourselves. Private sector unions organize plant by plant, so maybe schools, maybe districts, maybe even subjects, like the trades do. Open-shop, with teachers voluntarily paying dues to their unions, and participating as at-will members of a collective bargaining unit or not, as each individual person decides. If you have a good reason to join, then persuade folks, don't force it on them.

Local school boards should nullify all state and federal mandates and run their districts as they see fit. With a conservative governor and legislature and bunch of buzzed up tea-partiers raising heck, there will never be a more favorable time than right now to end the state funding formula and return to local funding and local control of schools. The elimination of the state-level bureaucracy and the cost of local compliance with state mandates will provide more funding for teachers' compensation, if local districts see the need. And teachers can teach – wouldn't that be refreshing. What's that? Obama won't stand for it? Hey – he's your guy, handle it.

Is there anyone in the world more keenly interested in the quality of education provided to the kids in each classroom their parents, their principal, and the teacher? Then why in the world did we ever turn that classroom over to a bureaucrat in Madison or Washington D.C. that has never, and will never, met a single one of those kids? Take it back – take back the money, take back the control, take back the responsibility. I have a cousin who teaches and a cousin who works at the Federal Department of Education. The former doesn't need the latter.

How much money do we need for education? $8,000 a kid, 30 to a class, that's $240,000. Give the teacher $120,000 and that leaves $120,000 for overhead. If you can't run a school for that, get out of the business. Do you still hate me, teachers? Has your WEAC leadership ever come close to giving you this kind of opportunity? And you don't even pay me dues.

Most Wisconsin school districts are within commuting distance of one or more other districts, so competition and choice among neighboring districts will establish something akin to a market for teachers where merit, not seniority or education level, will determine fair compensation. It works for welders, architects, nurses, accountants, engineers, salespeople, IT geeks; don't think you are so extra special, teachers - I went to school with you.

Teacher's pay should be set by their customers – the parents – through their elected local school board representatives with input from peers and school administrators. I don't know if you can convince parents to pay you $120k or not, but you didn't get anywhere this week by holding a sign and yelling at a building, now did you?

Best practices will soon spread and inequities between districts will not last very long. The best teachers will see their pay and benefits increase, and the worst teachers will be driven out of education into a field more suited to their talents and abilities. Communities with bad schools will not attract young families, and will not achieve economic growth. Communities with good

---

schools will become magnets for families and will prosper. The bad school communities will turn over their school boards and get somebody in there that will make things better and bring families (and property values and tax revenues and trade) to the community.

The time has come for unbridled school-choice. Parents should have the right to opt-out of the public school systems and select from a range of public or private options or home-school their kids if they want. If we make enough choices available – which a free market will do – then we can hold parents accountable for failing to educate their children. Right now, we hold nobody accountable, and it shows – we have lousy students, lousy teachers, lousy administrators, lousy parents, and lousy bureaucrats in faraway places making a lot of money and making things a lot worse.

Very poorly-run districts will have a hard time finding any teachers willing to work in them, and they will have to pay dearly until they get their situation under control. This will provide the incentive to actually get their situation under control. Go ahead and laugh, Milwaukee – nothing else any of you have tried for the past 50 years has worked. In every other industry, the largest competitors have the lowest cost and the highest quality – in education, it works exactly the opposite. Try it my way.

Finally, tenure has got to go. I know all of the theory about academic freedom, but in practice, it is a license for lazy and lousy teachers to remain that way with impunity. Without the protection of a forced-union monopoly and tenure, bad teachers will either become good or they will leave.

So there you go – a libertarian education reform plan that pays teachers more, educates children better, makes parents accountable for educating their kids, and relies on local control and market forces to improve the education system for everyone – everyone except the union bosses and bureaucrats who add no value.

Or, you can just keep writing nasty comments about the Governor all over the internet. Good luck with that.

Get On With It.

At the core of the dispute inflaming passions in Wisconsin this past week are two incompatible principles – Free Will versus Free Lunch. When Free Will said "no more" to Free Lunch, the stuff hit the fan. A week of it has not changed a mind, so let's just get on with it.

The unionists in America now have the same problem that unionists had in Poland decades ago - the State and its employee unions have become indivisible. The Solidarity movement in Poland fought for local independent union representation, and enjoyed support from across the political spectrum. If Wisconsin workers were fighting for this, they would find themselves widely supported, too.

But that is not what they are fighting for. The state unions are fighting to maintain their monopoly – a monopoly that that makes their hand a permanent fixture of the public cookie jar. The bakers of this state have decided this arrangement is no longer suitable. There are two million taxpayers in Wisconsin, and 175,000 tax-eaters on the public payroll. We all know how this will end.

It is ironic that health care, the spark that ignited the Tea Party movement – has suddenly inflamed the passions on the other side. Unionists object to the State forcing public workers to make a 12% contribution towards their health insurance; where was this outrage when the State imposed a 100% contribution on millions of citizens with ObamaCare? That was different; it was someone else's money.

And when they were pushing for universal national health care the Left argued it was unfair for government workers to have such better health insurance than the rest of Americans, remember? Turns out they don't really like fairness and equality all that much. For all the wailing they do about the income gap, they seem quite comfortable with their perch on the high side of the benefits gap.

As a matter of fact, the protests in Madison have pretty much laid to rest all of the Left's sanctimonious pretensions in one fell swoop. Equality? We have had a near riot over moving less than half-way to equality in benefits. Education? The educators walked off the job. Environment? Did you see the mountain of garbage they left behind them at the Capitol? Democracy? They ran to Illinois. Poverty? Women's issues? Did any of those $75k WEAC teachers offer to reimburse the $20k single moms for the extra days of day care imposed when teachers shut the schools down?

State workers now contend this whole dispute is not about the benefit concessions; rather it is about the denial of their right to representation in the workplace. Coincidentally, this change of position occurred within a few hours of the internet posting of each teacher's actual salary and benefits, but I give them the benefit of the doubt. A teachers-union friend of mine explained to me that government workers can not accept a ban on collective bargaining, as it would leave them with no protection from their employer.

Finally, something we can agree on; we libertarians have long argued that *all* Americans need to be protected from "their employer". It is vindication to hear that those know the government best - the people who make it up - don't feel safe within their own tribe of cannibals.

You may recall that Senator Chuck Schumer insisted "their employer" was needed to keep the private health care industry "honest". As it turns out, the people who would be performing this critical task don't even trust themselves to manage health care for themselves. Maybe now that state workers have taken the position that the government can not be trusted to serve the public good, we can start to dismantle the whole brutish enterprise and go back to living free.

Facts have been very difficult to come by in this last week of hysteria, but one of the least disputed - and least reported - is the fact that government workers spend twice as much as the rest of us on health care. That was an eye-opener.

The government-provided family plan costs the state $22,000 while a typical private sector family plan costs less than $12,000. Insurance rates in Dane County, home of both state government and University of Wisconsin, are dramatically higher than in the rest of the state as a consequence.

What are we to make of this? Are government workers twice as sickly as private sector workers? Are the plan negotiators for the government only half as good as their private sector counterparts? Do government workers pay twice as much for each MRI, or are they getting twice as many MRIs?

All those masters' degrees marching and cursing and generally losing it at the Capitol over a 12% contribution to their premiums might want to stop yelling long enough to ponder how it is their private sector counterparts spend 50% less for our medical care. I'll spare them the trouble; we spend less because we are not spending someone else's money. That is the difference between economics and arithmetic; you get to understand *why* the numbers come out the way they do.

Two years ago, liberals based their whole case for national Health Care Reform on the fact that "we" spend more than France does on health care. As it turns out, "we" don't spend more; our public sector unions spend more. They spend double what "we" spend, and there are so darn many of them now that it bends up the whole nation's infamous cost curve – the one our President likes to read about on his teleprompter.

But President Cost-Curve did not send Governor Walker a note congratulating him on taking actions that will make health care more affordable for all Wisconsinites. No, the President sent 25,000 of his elves to Wisconsin to try to insure that our public unions will *always* be able to spend twice as much on health care as the rest of us do and insure that we will *always* pay for their free lunch.

Estimates of the numbers of protestors this past weekend have been wildly distorted by both sides, as have the budget numbers and the facts about state educational performance. A friend sent me statistics that "proved" the five states without collective bargaining had terrible schools. While checking, I discovered that 8 of the top 20 public schools in USA today rankings – 40% - are located in these few supposedly "bad" states. Wisconsin – the good state - did not place one public school in the top 100.

And the best-rated public education is found where they spend the least – Utah.

And so it is with socialism and freedom. Freedom produces uneven excellence, and socialism produces equal mediocrity. No amount of protesting will change that – it has been proven over the centuries, across cultures, and in various economic settings – public education did not get a waiver from the laws of economics and the vagaries of human nature.

In the end, the numbers of protesters don't matter; it is the number of votes that were cast this past November that do. Governor Walker is fulfilling a campaign promise, and he won big on it. The state gave him a Republican legislature and senate to insure that he got it done.

That is what will happen, and the sooner the better. No one's mind will change in a week, or a month, or a year. Just get on with it, please.

CAPITALISTA!

Raging Against The Machine

Some days, this column writes itself. The first two news articles I read this morning were once again about the standoff in Wisconsin between taxpayers and tax-eaters, and I spent most of the commute still shaking my head in disbelief that this is not all a dream.

The first was an article was from the Milwaukee Journal Sentinel about the weekend's happenings in Madison – "ground zero", as they put it, for the protests against Governor Walker's plan to avoid thousands of layoffs by restricting collective bargaining for government workers.

Jesse Jackson showed up and so did the guy from Rage Against The Machine – the media liked that. Two women were quoted in the article while standing up for their rights; one was a 61 year old who retired after 20 years at the University of Wisconsin Department of Landscape Architecture. Another was a 30 year-old theater research doctoral student in her 6th year of labs.

Not even Woody Guthrie could make that into a protest song.

Don't get me wrong, I like to rage against the machine more than most guys my age, but it is frankly pretty hard to get your rage on against a machine that gives you a generous pension after 18 years of teaching theory of mulch and taking two sabbaticals. Maybe Rev. Jackson could have found something to rhyme with "theater research", but that would have taken longer than he stayed in town once the cameras were turned off.

Professional student at 30 and pensioner before 61 – this is what liberal media chose for the face of what's at stake here in Wisconsin. At first I thought it was an absurd irony, but upon reflection, these bookends capture the crux of matter perfectly: what the tax-eaters see as rights, the taxpayers see as a lifestyle they are no longer willing to fund.

The next article was at **www.wisn.com** about Milwaukee mayor Tom Barrett's predictably dire warnings if Governor Walker's plan passed. The Mayor said any state budget cuts would cause him to cut police and fire in the city's poorest communities, and he scolded the Governor for leaving the state's poorest residents unprotected, saying, "...a cut from state revenues is a cut to public safety."

It was the reporter's sentence after Barrett's quoted remarks that seal the deal, "Barrett also unveiled a plan to help revamp Wisconsin Avenue from the Milwaukee River to Marquette University."

For two weeks I have been begging to hear the Democrat alternative to Walker's budget fix and promising to post it here if someone would send it to me, so here it is: layoff workers and buy some art-deco lampposts. The Milwaukee mayor's ultimatums to the rest of Wisconsin's citizens - pay for my cops and firefighters or else – reminds us all why the phrase "or else" exists.

And speaking of no game...how is it that we have a couple dozen GOP peek-a-boo presidential candidates that all talk smack about fiscal discipline and taking on public sector unions, and standing with Walker, but when it's go-time only one – my friend Herman Cain – actually came here and stood with the man. Those Democratic state senators weren't the only ones avoiding Wisconsin.

For all of you tax-eaters that still don't get it, here is what's wrong with public sector unions: you can't be both the hand and the cookie jar.

In the private sector, union compensation is kept from spiraling out of control by the presence of other suppliers and customers who are free to choose. There is no other State of Wisconsin, and Eagle River doesn't have the option of joining Texas, although I know a few people up there who would like to give it a go.

The market forces that establish an environment for meaningful collective bargaining simply do not exist in the public sector and no amount of laws or signs or chants that start with "hey, hey, ho, ho," are going to change that. Unionists who insist on making the dispute over their entitlements a principled debate about rights come up about 66% short on that front.

CAPITALISTA!

In the workplace, the natural right of association has three component parts: the right to join a union and bargain collectively, the right to work free of union impairment, and the right of the employer to recognize or not recognize any collective bargaining unit. The Libertarian Party national platform plank on Labor Markets strongly supports all three dimensions of the constitutionally-protected right of association:

We support repeal of all laws which impede the ability of any person to find employment. We oppose government-fostered forced retirement. We support the right of free persons to associate or not associate in labor unions, and an employer should have the right to recognize or refuse to recognize a union. We oppose government interference in bargaining, such as compulsory arbitration or imposing an obligation to bargain.

No fence left to ride there. Nothing was settled today, and nothing will be settled tomorrow. Each day starts and ends with absurdities and ends with so many false claims the Truth-o-Meter guy will be the next to go on strike. Meanwhile 99% of us who have jobs are back to work or never left. That makes for really boring TV, though, so we will have to watch the paid chimps howl and flip at the Capitol for a while longer.

Proficiency

Here is the education story from Wisconsin this week that really matters: only 39% of eighth graders in the public schools are proficient in math, and only 34% in reading, despite a 65% increase in per-pupil spending over the past decade.

While the attention of the nation is focused on what Wisconsin teachers earn, the question of what they do to earn it has been largely ignored. What they do *not* do is educate our children.

Spare me the hate mail, teachers, as I will give you the first round – I will stipulate that you are all terrific and it is the system that prevents you from showing it. Now, you give me the second round, and admit that you are fighting tooth and nail to keep that awful system intact.

The public education system is operated under the work rules that have been collectively bargained; that is reason enough to end collective bargaining privileges. Education Secretary Arne Duncan called Wisconsin's proficiency results "unacceptable". He must not be proficient either, because not only does he accept them, but he and his boss have sent 25,000 shock troops to defend the system of forced unionization and collective bargaining that produced them in the first place.

Proficiency is the only purpose of education – not spending, not teachers' pay, not union representation, not pensions, not benefits, not political indoctrination, not PC speech, not stickers and stars for trying, not outcome equality, not coddling delinquent students, delinquent teachers, delinquent administrators, or delinquent parents.

Green Bay Packer cornerback Charles Woodson supported the protesting public union workers in Wisconsin, citing his own players' union as an example of how collective bargaining secures good wages for workers. We all love him in this state, but Mr. Woodson does not earn millions because he is a 34% proficient cornerback with a strong union behind him.

Mr. Woodson earns millions because he is exceptionally proficient. He got that way by working harder than his peers, by going the extra mile, by developing is distinctly unequal talent, by refusing to conform to the common denominator, by rejecting equality of outcome, and by taking heat from coaches who cared enough to push him to greatness. He does not share his excess speed with those less speedy, and he does not get paid on a seniority scale negotiated collectively by Mark Tauscher based on averaging their times in the 40.

Proficiency is the common denominator for all high-income earners; they are extremely proficient at what they do, whether it is Charles Woodson, Oprah Winfrey, the Koch brothers, George Soros, or Lady Gaga. Their compensation is determined by the value they add. Proficiency is how all compensation is determined in the private sector, from the busboy up to the CEO. Imperfectly, to be certain.

Few, if any, of Wisconsin's eighth graders are going to grow up and win the Heisman Trophy, host their own talk show, build a multi-billion dollar business, corner the markets on currency derivatives, or sell millions of dance records. Most of them will try to find a decent job in the private sector, where their earnings will be determined by their proficiency, and where we do not grade on the curve.

The engineer's calculations must be correct, not politically correct. The proposal writer can not thumb-type "OMG r u k w/price lol :-)" on company letterhead and expect that to win his firm a multi-million dollar bid. Nobody cares how the architect feels about her design that the client hated, the salesman does not get a chance to come back and improve his presentation, and your lawyer won't win your patent case because it's his turn. We don't all finish together in the real world.

Do the public schools prepare our children to survive and thrive in this world where their earnings will be determined by their proficiency? Clearly not. Wisconsin's middle class is not disappearing because one party or another is in a majority; it is disappearing because un-proficient people are not worth middle-class wages. But it is a lot easier to curse at capitalists and China than it is to face the truth.

Anyone who has actually been to China comes back with a fuller appreciation for the true nature of the economic threat posed by that rival nation. China is not a land of coulee labor chained to benches in dingy sweatshops hunched slaving over pennies for hours on end. China is mile after mile of gleaming new factories full of new high-technology equipment, clean as a clinic, efficient as all get-out, and full of energetic, smiling, young faces proud of their productivity and their rapid climb up the income scale.

Those factories were designed by Chinese industrial architects, and built by Chinese skilled tradesmen operating Chinese-made cranes and heavy equipment. The machines and assembly lines were designed by Chinese engineers and built by Chinese craftsmen. The skilled workers who operate and maintain the machinery are Chinese, the trainers are Chinese, the inspectors are Chinese, and the management is Chinese. The capital to invest in these productive factories is Chinese, the surplus product of a 50% savings rate; the banks that finance the development and working capital are Chinese.

All those smart, proficient Chinese people are the product of Chinese schools. Children start school at 7 years of age, and complete 9 years of compulsory education – 8 hours per day, 5 days a week, 10 months per year. 60% of curriculum is devoted to math and reading (Chinese). At the end of each school year, tests must be passed to advance to the next year. Teachers must have a 2-year certificate to teach, and local boards control local schools.

Students who do not grasp lessons stand in front of the class to be tutored by the teachers and other students until they learn. Parents are required to come to school and take notes when children are ill. The expectation is that every single child will learn to be fully proficient, and they are. A University of Michigan study reported that Chinese students perceive the classroom as competitive and teacher-controlled and they are happy about it. Proficient people are happy people.

Our public education industry would – and do - say they are doing it all wrong over in China. And when Chinese students placed 1st in math and reading comprehension in last year's standardized PISA testing, while the U.S. ranked 31st in math and 17th in reading, our educators scoffed at the very notion that their work could be measured by testing. Arne Duncan told us that teaching was not the cause of our dismal showing, admonishing us that "it's complicated."

Yes, it is clearly too complicated for Secretary Duncan and the public education industry, who have ruined our public school system by turning it into a social science laboratory experiment gone horribly wrong. That is exactly why they should not be allowed to run it any more.

But it is apparently not too complicated for the Chinese, nor was it too complicated for our parents and grandparents and several previous generations of Americans who managed to do make us proficient at a fraction of the cost, without the benefit of our modern technology, and without collective bargaining for benefits and work rules.

We are Americans; and we can beat the Chinese, because freedom was invented here, and only copied there. Choice and competition will save our schools, and saving our schools will save our kids, and saving our kids will save our state and our nation so that generations of Americans can all live free and prosper. That's why Wisconsin matters.

Taxeaters

Welcome to the second Civil War. This time it is the taxpayers against the taxeaters; the hand versus the cookie jar. The tea party sparked it, Governor Chris Christie of New Jersey declared it, and now Governor Scott Walker of Wisconsin has fired the first shot.

On one side of the economic Mason/Dixon line are taxpayers, people who send more money to government than they receive from it. On the other is taxeaters, whose ledger balance is reversed. Pick your side, either by circumstance or by aspiration or by affection.

And then pace yourself, as we all have a very long ways to go. All of the towns in all of the counties in all of the states across the country are broke, and so is the federal government that has been bailing them all out for the past 40 years with borrowed money. They all have to balance their own budgets, and there is no cavalry coming.

I heard the first warning that this day would come when I was 10 years old in 1964; I had no idea what "untenable" meant back then, but I sure get it now. And balancing government budgets means cutting spending, because there is no more money – our taxpayers won't give any more, and the Chinese won't lend any more.

Meanwhile, our federal government is a week or so away from a shutdown. Taxeaters are apoplectic over the thought, while taxpayers are crossing off the days on our calendars. For libertarians, it will be a holiday – I Told You So Day.

No one will die; most of what is shut down will not even be noticed. The government will have to spend only what it takes in, and spend it only on essential services. Air traffic controllers will be on duty, and the NPR grant won't make the cut. Belgium is on day 250 of their government shutdown and they still live longer than us. Breathe, breathe.

Just like our first one, our second civil war is also about slavery. The first time, we emancipated others in the private sector; this time we are emancipating ourselves from the public sector. Ok, technically, we are not tax slaves, rather indentured servants. The difference is that indentured servants can theoretically end their slavery by paying off the debt owed to their master.

And what is that debt up to these days? According to USA Today, our government is facing $63.8 trillion of debt obligations – sovereign debt, pension liability, entitlement obligations, health care, and so on. Your household's share is $546,888. That is not a misprint; that is what the taxeaters' spending habits have racked up on your dime. That's why we aren't getting along so good these days.

I hope this post will reach some of you 20-year-old college students who joined the public unions to protest in Madison these past weeks, because your $546,888 share works out to installments of $29,956 per year for the next 50 years. You were marching with the people who don't think that is enough – did you know that? And every day we don't fix our budget problems the pile gets $4 billion deeper.

This is serious stuff, the kind that serious people are trying to fix, while unserious people continue to lie, sloganeer, pitch a fit, or just run away.

When you students were hauling signs around for the greybeards at Bitch Fair On The Square, your solidarity brothers and sisters probably didn't tell you that you will have to work past 70 so they can keep on retiring in their 50's, did they? I didn't think so.

And they probably just forgot to tell you that you will earn only half of what they do in real dollars as the mountain of debt devalues our currency over your lifetime. And I'm certain they did not mention that the collective bargaining they insist on is how we got union-owned health insurance that costs team taxpayer $10,000 more than what insurance costs private employers on the open market.

How much of that ten grand per worker do you suppose goes straight from the taxpayer's wallet to the taxeaters' unions, the source of most Democrat campaign funds? Now do you understand why they were throwing cups and papers when the law past in the lower chamber last night? Do you see why the idea that a donor could buy a governor for paltry $43k is insulting to someone with intelligence and a basic grasp of how things really work in the tawdry world of money and politics.

This is your future we're talking about; use your head. Want to guess which side was bought off with donor money? How about the one wearing their donor's T-shirts, for Pete's sake? Of course they went hysterical – just like Lindsay Lohan when the judge ordered her to rehab. The party's over and they can already feel the shakes coming on. They told disabled people they would die if the bill passed - you can't even look up and see the bottom of the barrel from that place.

Your household's $546,888 isn't enough for the taxeaters; they want more. And don't forget you will be picking up their $546,888 shares too, because taxeaters get their money from you, the taxpayer. The most honest thing said about the intent of these protests was the union guy who threatened to anal rape the gay camera man – we have been taking it there for half a century from these mugs.

As you students contemplate the complicated issues of fiscal policy and social justice I ask you to at least consider this: you are only one graduation day and one hire date away from those Capitol protests changing from being about *the* money to being about *your* money. This is all about how much you are willing to take from your wallet and give to those people hollering in the rotunda. The Governor does not have a big box of cash that gets filled up by the tooth fairy every night for him to give out to everyone that wants some.

You are taxeaters right now, but you are about to move over to the other side of the table for the rest of the dinner party at the cannibals' house. Hopefully, you will all get good jobs so you can be in the upper half of income earners; that is why you went to school. We top 50% income earners pay 96% of the taxes - that's the machine you were raging against last week. The taxeaters have their thongs all twisted in a bunch since November because we said no to the other 4%.

Ours is the jersey you will put on pretty soon; and when you do, then all those mean, vile, vicious threats that the taxeaters hurled at us last week will be directed at you. You will be the problem, the greedy one, the enemy of democracy because you do not give them more of your money. Don't take it personal, it's just their quirky way of telling us how much they love and appreciate us for paying all their doctor bills when their children get sick. You're welcome, taxeaters.

Now, of course you can give the taxeaters more of your money, there is absolutely nothing preventing you from paying more taxes than you owe if you think higher taxes are a good answer for our budget problems. Actually paying more would make you stand out in the crowd of liberals who say I should, but never do themselves.

Public sector workers hate to be called taxeaters; they argue that they are taxpayers too. Well, not really. When your daughter rebates you 10% of her allowance she does not join you as a breadwinner; she becomes a bit less of a burden in strictly economic terms, and this is economics, not social studies. Of course we love our daughters, just like we love our teachers and cops and city clerks, but we eventually have to say no more Justin Bieber posters for you, sweetie, because Daddy ran out of money. Some kids pout longer than others.

This is not a game, and it's not about the political class of Republicans and Democrats or their fawning media cheerleaders keeping the applause lights lit. It is about your liberty, your economic opportunity, your prosperity, your future. History is replete with the cases of great nations which have collapsed under the weight of the debt they have run up to appease their taxeaters' demands.

It will happen here if we do not quickly and drastically change course. That will not be easy and it will not be painless. It will just be less painless than staying on course and going over the cliff.

Madison Wild Wings

In a response to my piece entitled, "Taxeaters", a reader who favored progressive income taxation posed this question back to me: why *shouldn't* the top 50% of income earners pay 96% of the taxes?

My answer: for the same reason that they shouldn't have to pick up 96% of the state's collective bar tab. All knowledge builds upon what you know.

That evening, I pondered his question some more and was inspired while enjoying a pub meal that Michelle Obama would ban if she could. And here is the problem with progressive income tax theory played out a fictional place called Madison Wild Wings.

Let's say there are 200 tables at MWW and the bill for each is $100 for a total of $20,000. The manager announces a better, fairer way to pay the bill - progressive, he calls it. Sounds like progress, so the customers go along, and besides they are watching the Badgers on the big screens and not paying much attention.

He sorts the tables by income into the 100 lower-half tables and the 100 upper-half tables. We'll call the upper-half "taxpayers" and the lower-half "taxeaters", just because it drives liberals nuts when I do that.

He then informs the upper 50% - the taxpayers – that their share of the total MWW bill for the night is 96%, or $19,200. There are 100 tables, so they each must pay $192 for their $100 of food. The taxeaters share is $800 or $8 per table. The servers get 20% tips from each table, so some make $38.40 and some making $1.60, which creates MWW's first-ever income gap.

Is this fair? According to liberals, the United States government, and all but handful of states that have no income tax, the answer is a resounding "yes!" Is it smart? We will find out on Day 2 of the progressive payment plan at Madison Wild Wings.

Day 2: The crowd is a little different tonight; can you guess how? Right, there are more taxeaters and fewer taxpayers. And the taxeaters order the best of everything now that they know someone else is paying. The total bill surges to $30,000.

Taxpayers' share is $28,880 – $280 per table - while the taxeaters pay just $12 per table for $150 of appetizers, entrées, dessert, and blender drinks. The servers on the taxpayer side got $56 tips per table, while the taxeaters got $2.40, so all the best servers go work the taxpayer side.

Are the taxeaters grateful to the taxpayers? No – in fact, they are furious that their bill went up 50% from $8 to $12! Plus their service was horrible, because their servers suck at it. They accuse the manager of ripping off poor people, and then call him racist and homophobe for good measure, even though he is gay and Hispanic. The bad servers form a union - the I Hate Rich People Union.

A University professor with a Ph.D. gets a grant to study the problem. He asks the taxeaters if they have been screwed by rich people; they say yes, they have been screwed by rich people; he concludes they have been screwed by rich people. That wins him a Nobel Prize, and President Obama makes him a Czar of some new agency that will tell MWW how to make wings from now on. Dr. Duh funnels federal grants to his old University and they name a building after him. The sandal people are pleased.

The MWW manager doesn't want to lose most of his customers, so he agrees to tax the rich even more, increasing their share to 98%. This is quite popular with the taxeaters. He also donates to President Obama's campaign and gets a waiver from ObamaCare.

Day 3: Even more taxeaters show up, some bussed up from Illinois, just like their parents did in the 70's, the last time there were free wings in Wisconsin. Some taxpayers quit working and join the taxeaters side, some go elsewhere; there are only 50 tables filled in the upper half. And the bill comes to $40,000 this time. Ben Bernanke reports this increase a 33% rise in GDP. Ron Paul laughs at him.

98% means the taxpayers have to pay $39,200 and since there are only 50 tables, each table's share shoots up to $784. The taxeaters total share is $800, back to just $8 per table. Except now the servers on the taxeater side go on strike because their tips dropped back down from $2.40 to $1.60 per table. Ben Bernanke adjusts GDP downward and Paul Krugman blames the strike on greedy rich people.

Then Bernanke remembers that you can't spend the same dollar twice, so $39,200 of something else won't get bought somewhere else, and he has to adjust GDP all the way back to zero. This confuses Joe Biden, so he just calls it 12,000 new stimulus jobs and asks directions to that custard place.

By now everybody at MWW is angry. Taxeaters are complaining, taxpayers are leaving, the servers are on strike, the kitchen help is going back to Mexico, managers are quarrelling, profits are down, Ben Bernanke is testy, the cost for taxpayers to eat at MWW are more than double any other wing joint in town, and Joe Biden is still there and won't shut up.

Note to students: this is what we mean by the term "hostile business climate". At Madison Wild Wings it is bad – one of the 10 worst in the nation. New taxpaying customers peek inside and run away to spend their evening somewhere more hospitable.

Meanwhile over at the Texas, Tennessee, and Florida Dutch Treat Wing Emporium, the place is packed with taxpayers who fled from MWW, along with the best servers who can earn more without the union. The TTFDTWE is profitable, the patrons are happy, the servers are making good money, and taxpayers and taxeaters are back comingled at their tables, laughing and getting along just fine. Prices are low and dropping, quality is high and improving, and the menu is expanding with more choices every day. Capitalists and libertarians are not surprised, because everyone is acting in their own self interest and of their own free will.

Note to students: this is what will happen when Wisconsin passes Right To Work legislation. That is how you fix a hostile business climate.

CAPITALISTA!

Back to our story...the progressives are shocked and appalled by TTFDTWE. Someone on WPR sniffs back tears and calls it the Walmart of NASCAR Waffle Houses, and the next caller claims she is David Koch and says the whole state of Arizona is a bleepin' MubarakDictatorBushHitler. The sandal people whisper-talk their glee at her clever gotcha, saying, "right on" and "solid" and "word". They don't understand the meaning of "word", but it sounds really, really black.

Day 4: Now the taxeaters demand free high speed rail to take them to MWW and back, and they want free health care. The taxpayer side at MWW starts drinking tea and fighting back. The old manager abruptly retires to Spain after taking a lavish Cancun vacation and buying some train cars. The till is empty when the new manager shows up for work, and his bookkeeper tells him the budget is in the red by $3.3 billion.

He meets the taxpayers, who politely remind him who pays his salary and then give him a folded note with a message for the taxeaters. The new manager walks over to the taxeaters, and opens the note and calmly says, "The people who pay my salary have asked me to tell you to buy your own damn wings."

The taxeaters go berserk, walk off their jobs, take over the state Capitol, hide in Illinois... Well, you know the rest of the story; we have been living it for real in Wisconsin for three ugly weeks now. It is fitting that the cradle of the progressive movement is also the cemetery in which it will be buried, and someone needs to pull the plug on this ridiculous life-support stalemate of a protest the unionists have inflicted.

The progressive income tax is not simply bad economic policy, it is inherently immoral. If you only earn 10 times more than me, why should you pay 30 times more in taxes? Because you have it and I want it? That is the morality of the brute, the rapist, the looter, and yes, the taxeater. The 10% tithe in religion is a voluntary flat-rate revenue source, and personally, I would choose God over socialists when it comes to moral imperatives and questions of infallibility.

For the past century, socialist progressives have wrapped their turd of an ethos with the plight of the poor, the infirmed, the children, the disenfranchised, and even the planet; hoping their faux-compassionate veneer would distract us from the stench.

Like most other things, they are wrong. And so is their progressive income tax.

Feelings

The libertarian argument for radically limited government has never been more eloquently made than by the nationwide protests over public unions and collective bargaining.

Not that the protestors are on our side; anything with "compulsory" or "collective" is presumptively anti-libertarian, and compulsory collective bargaining is near the top of our list of dangerous substances.

Rather, they have illustrated, with great clarity, the fundamental incompatibility between freedom and government. It is the love of the former and the fear of the latter that defines the libertarian. It is the love of the government and the fear of liberty that defines the statist.

The protests which continue across the nation remind me of an outpouring of the uncontainable rage of a jilted lover; statists see the government they adore is leaving them, and they are inconsolable. Hell hath no fury, so the saying goes, and the pleadings behind the signs and placards might as well read, "if you leave me I will die", "if I can't have you no one will", "I gave up everything for you", and "your new girlfriend is a whore". A whore with a Hitler mustache drawn on it.

This has nothing to do with rights, and everything to do with feelings. To describe the public unions' protests against fiscal austerity as an uprising of people against the state shows an appalling ignorance of the terms "people" and "state".

The War for Independence was fought by the people *against* the state; its purpose was to liberate American citizens from unbearable taxation, unjustifiable intrusion into private matters, and the stifling of reforms by employees of a distant government.

Today's protests are lodged on *behalf* of the state; their purpose is to defend the state against the people, to maintain unbearable taxation and intrusive bureaucracies, and to block reform by moving legislators to foreign jurisdictions.

In the 1960's, large-scale protests were organized to fight *against* coercion – the war, the draft, discriminatory laws, voter disenfranchisement, drug prohibition, and other institutional deprivations of individual rights.

Today's large-scale protests are organized to *protect* coercion – compulsory unionization, confiscatory taxation, overreaching regulation, and voter disenfranchisement by legislative abdication.

Four decades ago, the generation that is now marching to protect its state-monopoly privilege was marching against the ever-expanding power of the state; today they *are* the state.

The state is not some inanimate object; a set of books and buildings separate and distinct from the people in its employ; the state is nothing more than the people it employs. Our liberty can't be confiscated by vans with state-owned on the license plates; it is the people in the vans who do the taking. When the vans are empty, they cannot hurt us. It is the people who left them to march that intend to do us harm. Anyone who still doubts that has not been paying attention.

Thomas Sowell called it "the right to win", when he described the perverse and unshakable belief on the left that they are entitled to rule over us. That is the only "right" that is being fought over on the streets of our capitals this winter.

Tens of thousands of statists did *not* come out to protest the continuing wars halfway around the globe. When the previous Governor ignored both the U.S. and Wisconsin Constitutions to ban open carry, or when medical marijuana was outlawed again, or when a $1 billion tax increase was levied on the people without a minute of floor debate, there was not a peep from the so-called civil libertarians on the left.

It was only when their own privileged status was tweaked that they took to the streets by the tens of thousands. Actions betray words.

The libertarian argument for limited government is both principled and practical. Those who still hope for government solutions to every problem need look no farther than the

CAPITALISTA!

Wisconsin Capitol, where government is not even competent to eject unlawful trespassers, armed with crock-pots, from its own buildings. It is ridiculous to imagine it might have better luck if we gave it something more complicated to do.

That is the end of your job interview, but your skills do not match our requirements, Mr. State; thank you very much for coming in today – don't call us, we'll call you.

The current budget crisis facing nearly every unit of government is a problem of basic arithmetic – adding and subtracting. Spending must be cut to equal revenue. But the statists answer to the math quiz is an essay; an endless boring essay that turns into a harangue and finally a threat when it does not get its way.

To all who have fought so vociferously against all of the Governors and Mayors and School Superintendents and County Executives on the issue of collective bargaining "rights" and public sector compensation, we all know how you feel. Now either answer a numeric question with a numeric answer, or shut up.

Collectively, the states and municipalities have a $122 billion math problem, and the federal government's is $1.5 trillion. Public sector workers know better than anyone how to reduce spending and balance budgets. What is your answer, and show us your work.

Give Me Liberty

If nothing else, the last month has made the argument for concealed carry in the state of Wisconsin. We now know the quickness at which angry mobs can turn predatory, and we now know how ineffective police protection can be.

I dare say that the jackal packs swarming Sen. Glen Grothman, or punching Fox reporters, or assaulting stranded opponents would not be so brazen if the prospect of their prey packing heat had to be factored into the threat calculus.

If anger leads to certain gun violence, then the 50,000 pissed-off unionists stomping around Capitol Square would have unleashed Armageddon. If vigilante justice is inevitable, then the 3 million pissed off taxpayers would have put down this whole childish tantrum after about a week of it. Neither one happened.

People who live in the country know they are on their own to defend themselves, their loved ones, and their property. Now city people have gotten a little taste of what it's like to be in surrounded by wild animals and no law enforcement officer with ten miles. The grinning fools in the uniforms giving the coyotes in the rotunda the thumbs up do not qualify – it's the part about enforcing the law that exposed them as law enforcement imposters.

Country people grow up with guns, and we give them about as much thought as the carving knife in the kitchen or the chain saw in the garage – dangerous if not used properly, necessary for the purposes intended.

There is no doubt that lots of guns were down on the square over the past month; the rounds of ammunition found inside the capitol building once the squatters were evicted did not surprise anyone. Walker supporters tend to be gun-friendly, and it is difficult to imagine that all went to their counter rally defenseless and outmanned by paid agitators from out of state.

Shots fired? Zero.

CAPITALISTA!

Wisconsin law explicitly allows for open carry of a firearm, a right – a real right, by the way – guaranteed by both the U.S. and the Wisconsin Constitutions. Can you imagine what kind of hell would have been unleashed if the Capitol Police would have arrested anyone for disturbing the peace with open carry, after refusing to enforce the law on the illegal occupation of the Capitol building itself?

The argument that guns provoke violence was disproven once and for all by the absence of gun violence during the heated protests in Wisconsin. There was plenty of other law-breaking.

As Ted Nugent said, a free person does not need a permission slip in order to defend himself. People who dislike guns are under no compulsion to buy one; but they have no right to deny the rights of others who choose to own and carry whatever means of self-defense they deem appropriate.

I'm Ok, You're Not Ok

A popular book on Transactional Analysis entitled, "I'm Ok, You're Ok" sold millions of copies when it came out in 1969. A lot of us baby boomers just read the title; we took it as a permission slip to do whatever we wanted. That's pretty much our signature move.

We created our own delusional definition of liberty – freedom from consequence – and built an entire ideological framework to support it. It was a shaky lattice constructed of moral relativism, cultural diversity, notional entitlement, positive collective "rights", the nanny state, subjugation of individual rights, perpetual debt, and the decoupling of status from achievement.

After nearly a month of unionist protests in Wisconsin and across the nation, it should be clear to even us boomers that the time has come to grow up and admit that some of us, sadly, are not ok.

For example, the people who vandalized the Capitol building - not ok. And the teachers who took their classrooms to the protest - not ok. Workers who walked off the job - not ok. Cops who refused to enforce the law - not ok. Doctors who wrote fraudulent permission slips - not ok. People who took their protests to opponents' private residences - not ok. The bomb-threat guy – not ok.

People who slung profanity and hate speech at public rallies in public places with children were present - not ok. The guy with sign proposing gang-rape of female news reporters - not ok. The self-titled feminists whose silence on that matter was deafening - not ok. Threatening anal rape of a gay camera man - not ok. The silence of the LGBT community on that one - not ok. The legislator in a union T-shirt threatening to kill another legislator - not ok. The silence from the members of that union - not ok.

And the media covering all of this ugliness like it was a conference of angels blocking a foreign dictator from microwaving American kittens on Wisconsin soil - not ok.

CAPITALISTA!

We have become a not-ok nation. Most of us have come to expect someone else will pick up the tab, clean up the mess, rebuild from the rubble, and catch us when we fall. When 90% of us carried the misfortunate 10% to a life of quiet dignity, that was ok. When 50% of us are carrying the other 50% to a life of arrogant privilege and noisy ingratitude, that is not ok.

There is unfortunately only one budget proposal for us to consider in Wisconsin, and it balances the budget with $4.2 billion in spending cuts. The smarter alternative from the leftist elites, who ridicule Governor Walker for his lack of a University degree, is...oh, that's right, nothing.

A million brainiacs with enough degrees to trigger a solar flare and all they can come up with is a collective pout delivered in four-syllable word diatribes and four-letter word tantrums. Duh, winning.

Even us wacky Libertarians can improve on the GOP plan without getting sweaty: add up the costs of incarceration, prosecution, and street enforcement of simple possession, and tell me again this is the best we can do. Or how about this: repeal *all* the tax loopholes and subsidies, instead of just the ones that Republicans don't like. How about School Choice? Nullification, anyone?

Democrats never did have game; they yell like Tarzan and play like Jane. Their guy "fixed" his budget gaps by robbing trust funds, raising taxes, reneging on debts, misappropriating stimulus money, and accounting voodoo. He gave out more silly tax breaks to his friends than Walker has friends. When it was their turn, the Democrats now hiding in Illinois did nothing, unless you want to count the smoking ban. That seems to be a recurring theme – doing nothing.

Would you not-ok people like this Governor to punt, too? How about he raids that $66 billion in the state employee pension trust fund? Since Michael Moore says that all money is a national resource, maybe Walker should just withdraw $4.2 billion of everybody's money from the fund and avoid all this unpleasantness.

Or how about he sells off state lands to mining and logging companies, so funding could be restored for mandatory recycling? And how much of a tuition increase did you sit-in student protestors volunteer so the University faculty won't have to pay 12% of their flu shot? Oh, that's right, nothing – it's your default setting.

Let me explain balancing a budget to all the faux-mensas out there who majored in social sciences or victimhood studies: you either spend less or you pay more.

It's a simple math problem; and I hate to break it to you, but "effin" is not a number. $4.2 billion works out to $2,366 per household, excluding the disabled and those below poverty line. If you don't want to cut spending, then just attach your check to the Recall Walker petition; no, double it to $4,732 since the Walker voters have already made their preference for spending cuts quite clear.

Better yet, have a telethon on Wisconsin Public Radio to raise the $4.2 billion in voluntary tax contributions; there's a nice libertarian solution to your partisan standoff. Let all the people of Wisconsin decide how much spending they want "spared" with their contributions, instead of running countless polls rigged to come out either against or in favor of the Governor's plan. How far do you think that campaign would get - a million dollars, maybe? Half that?

And there is the problem distilled to its essence: the not-ok people demand more government than they are willing to pay for. After decades of just going along with the flow, the ok people have decided not to give them any more of either one – government or money.

Every dollar that government spends is either a right or pork, depending on whether you are the butcher or the hog. All across the nation, the ok people have decided we do not want to be the hog anymore, and the not-ok butcher is angry about having to learn a new trade.

And if you happen to read this, Mr. Moore, the wealth you recently described as a national resource is actually the most personal thing there is. It is the warehouse that stores value between the time you labor and the time you consume. If it is not yours, then neither is your person or your pantry, the source and use of the wealth you find so troubling – except for your own $50 million, of course.

You, sir, are definitely not ok.

Union Busting

While the Wisconsin media continues to obsess over the partisan standoff between Republicans and Democrats in Madison, the many other fronts in the war between the taxpayers and the taxeaters has received only glancing coverage.

Idaho, Utah, Indiana, Ohio, Pennsylvania, New Jersey, New York, and Vermont (yes, that Vermont) have all taken measures to shrink the size of their public sector unions or to restrict collective bargaining privileges. Senator Jim DeMint (R-SC) has introduced federal Right-To-Work legislation which would guarantee all Americans in every state the right to work free of union impairment.

Unionists, statists, and most liberals decry all of these measures as "union-busting". While most who oppose unions try to wiggle out from underneath the charge, I wear that label with pride.

Damn right we should bust them; just like we should bust all the other economic monopolies and cartels. Unions could not even exist without the exemptions from federal anti-trust laws that their dirty campaign money has purchased.

Compulsory collective bargaining – key word compulsory – is incompatible with the principle of liberty. End of argument.

If union enthusiasts would simply make membership voluntary, I would be out there stomping around with them. But the "right" they insist upon is the right to deny the rights of others by force, and libertarians don't swim in that end of the pool, sorry.

Whenever there is a barrier that prevents the exercise of a civil right, it *should* be busted. Every American has the right to work – period. It is the most basic of civil rights, to own your person and the fruits of your labors. Nobody has the moral authority to deny you your person - nobody. Right To Work is no more complicated than its title; it is the denial of that right through forced-union privilege that requires tortured justifications.

Libertarians and conservatives are allies on Right To Work; this does not arise from a perfectly shared vision of a just society, rather from our common reverence for the Constitution. Where in the foundational documents is the principle that one right can be imposed by the state at the expense of two other co-equal rights? Where in the Constitution is the authority granted to government to force a person to pay a third-party tribute as a condition of employment? Show it to me.

You have a right to vote, and you are not forced to purchase that right from me. You have a right to speak, and you are not forced to purchase it from me. You have a right to worship, and you are not required to purchase it from me. You have a right to bear arms, and you are not required to purchase it from me. You have a right to due process, and you are not required to purchase it from me.

But when it comes to your right to work, in 28 states you *are* required to purchase it from me, as long as I call myself the amalgamated brotherhood or fraternal order of whatever, and persuade 50% of your co-workers – once, and by any means necessary - to pay the toll. And there's the rub.

In the past, you had to pay a poll tax to a political party to exercise the right to vote; in forced-union states, you still you must pay a tribute to the parent company of a political party in order to exercise your right to work. The second case is no less corrupt and reprehensible than the first, but many who marched against the former offense in their bell-bottomed days are now marching to protect the latter offense in their loose-fit years.

The civil rights movement of the 1960's busted the hold of the Ku Klux Klan over the Democratic Party in the South and abolished the poll tax. Right To Work in the 2010's will bust the unions' even more powerful stranglehold on the Democratic Party in the north, and abolish the workplace toll. Busting organizations whose sole purpose is to deny civil rights to others is a worthy and noble cause. Klan buster, trust buster, crime buster, union buster; it's all good.

It is the liberals who defend forced-union legislation that have the explaining to do. They have abandoned their commitment to civil rights, trading their principles for box seats in the game of political power and control. To continue to call themselves civil libertarians is dishonest. They are civil rights sellouts, and we should not be squeamish about calling them on it just because they are nice.

On one hand, they insist on a right for gay people to marry, but they would deny those same married gay people the right to work. They claim to be the defenders of women's rights in the workplace, yet categorically deny women their most basic workplace right – the right to work. They claim to be the protector of children, yet work tirelessly to deny children the right to work when they grow up. The advocates for workers with disabilities will not lift a finger to help the disabled work free of union impairment.

They will yell themselves hoarse over a 5% minority religion's potential offense over a mural with the Ten Commandments; but they find it perfectly acceptable to force the 49% of a workforce that voted against union membership to join it anyway and for employers to withhold the dues that will be used against their interests.

There are some of us who have concluded that the mobbed-up extortionists with initials on their windbreakers are vile; and we don't believe we should be coerced into joining their ranks by the government that represents us. That wacky notion is called freedom of association. If you think it is a proper role of government to force people into associations against their will, all I can say is that you should thank your lucky stars that I am not the Governor of your state.

It now seems clear that the unionists strategy in Wisconsin is to disenfranchise the whole state and nullify the November elections by keeping 14 Democratic State Senators in Illinois long enough to mount a nationally-orchestrated recall effort in selected Republican districts. That is our President's impaired vision of representative democracy in a republic.

There are over 5 million citizens in the state of Wisconsin. The vast majority of us do not live and breathe politics 24/7/365. We like to stay generally informed, and then every two years, we would like to weigh in on the performance of our representatives and the direction of our state. Then we want to get back to important things like business, work, family, church, clubs, charities, neighbors, friends, entertainment, romance, hobbies, intellectual pursuits, music, education, and sports, sports, sports.

But there is a tiny little minority who think they are so bloody important that they should hold the entire state hostage to their partisan sparring and self-absorbed tantrums. Their arrogance and condescension would be infuriating if we weren't so bored with it.

They think their passions are more important than ours. They think their uses for our money for are more important than our own. They think the perks of their own jobs are more important than the hundreds of thousands that won't be created here now that they have shown potential employers that we are a state run by folks that have either lost their minds or are losing their nerve.

They have a right to their opinions. But far more importantly, the rest of us have a right to work. And this would be a good time for the new government that was elected last fall to protect our rights to show us the respect of actually doing it. Right To Work – right now.

Job Creation

Wisconsin Governor Scott Walker is wrong. There, now all you statists can quit calling me a Republican scab. I don't mind the scab part, but I'm not a Republican, even though I could sell a lot more books that way.

A friend of a friend commented on one of my recent posts, challenging the Governor's claim that the Budget Repair Bill (BRB) would create 250,000 jobs. I read the bill from start to finish and there is no provision that would create any government jobs, so that much is true.

If the Governor did indeed say he would create 250,000 jobs, he is dead wrong, because governments cannot create jobs any more than governments can create citizens.

Job creation is like procreation; the less government interference, the better the chance of success, and the more enjoyable the experience. Just imagine if the state of Wisconsin set out to "create" 250,000 new citizens the way it "helps" businesses create new jobs.

First, you and your partner would have to incorporate, then apply for some permits, buy a license, register for all the child taxes to come, and demonstrate your "credentials". Put some of those TSA scanners to use. Some board in Madison will send you a letter telling you if you are adequate or not; there's a self-esteem builder.

Then you must present your "construction" plans, with detailed diagrams, maps, dynamic loading calculations, schedules, budgets, and specifications - the list of wine, dinner settings, mood music, candles, along with their countries of origin and union-made certifications.

If a commission approves your idea for making another citizen, you then must conduct an environmental impact study to make sure that you will not disturb any wetlands in the process. You will have to buy a helmet and some other safety gear before you get started – there is a pamphlet and a class. The feds will want a mitigation plan to reduce the added CO_2 emissions bought on by all that additional exhaling when the new citizens are created.

Then there would be hearings – endless hearings. A bunch of people you have never met will try to stop you from creating your new citizens. They will claim that your citizens will make their cows go barren, that your little babies will do evil and vile things to the planet, or crush the middle class, or that you will cause a slug to become extinct. Guaranteed you will disturb some heritage site or burial mound, even if you propose to create your new citizens in your own van. And lawsuits – you won't believe. You estimate your legal bills and choke down hard but decide to plow ahead and make some more Badgers anyway.

If you received any state incentives to help you purchase anything to get you started with your intimate little project, there will be all kinds of stings attached and you will be filling out progress forms and having auditors come to check them the whole time you are procreating. Don't worry - they will be too bored to watch; they are on the clock.

Then your tax accountant shows up to explain how things work down the road a bit. The more kids you have the more you will pay in taxes, fees, state insurances, dues, and licenses. All sorts of new mandates kick in as you expand your family from one to many children – small families get punished for becoming big families. Hey, if you can afford all those kids, you can pay a lot more in taxes, you greedy fat cat.

Meanwhile, the President is berating you for not creating more citizens, for sitting on your...um...assets. Michael Moore declares war on your family, and claims your children are a national resource – selfishly, because then he can eat them without paying sales tax. Jesse Jackson says a prayer asking his God to protect the world from you.

The Department of Workforce Development pays you a little visit and dumps a few dozen binders with all the laws and regulations you must follow in your household – minimum allowance, acceptable and unacceptable chores, notices of rights that must be posted on the bunk beds, numbers to call for your kids to file complaints you, ADA mandates, all the rules for discrimination and harassment that you have to follow – things like that.

The neighborhood bully stops by to drops off signature cards for your kids to join his union. The law says you have to let him talk to your kids, but you are prohibited from telling them the truth when he lies about all the candy they will get and how late they can stay up playing PS4, once they join up with the Amalgamated Brotherhood of Kidsters. The NLRB starts cranking out ginned-up unfair labor practices that go right to the press first, then to you. Your wife quits talking to you.

If half of your kids vote to join the union, then you can't talk to any of them anymore. You must negotiate all the household rules with the bully and give him the money withheld from your children's allowance. When he doesn't get what he wants out of you, he calls the state in to investigate trumped up safety violations, unhealthy practices, and violations of the living contract he forced you to accept or lose your kids. You get fined and the papers print all sorts of bad things about you that are not true. Creating citizens sure is difficult.

So you are pondering where to create more citizens, and you wonder if that bully can really come between you and my kids like that without the state coming in to protect you. And then you watch him order an entire Party caucus of Senators to leave the state, and then you watch him call in the goons from Illinois to ransack the state capital, make death threats, boycott businesses, and hurl profanities at you.

You watch him yank state workers off their jobs and teachers out of the classroom and you realize the vandals who are breaking and entering and intimidating anyone who disagrees with them are the same folks who will be regulating your growing family. You watch the police assist the looters, you watch the mayors join the protests, and you realize those are the people you will call for help when the Children of the Corn come for your kids. This is how they act when they are out of power, and you are never more than one election away from having no one around to stop them.

Can't wait to create more citizens here? That is why job creators have been leaving northern forced-union states and moving to southern and western Right-To-Work states in recent decades.

How many more will have to leave before the taxeaters who haven't had an original thought since the 1920's will get it?

Government does not create jobs; that is the point that liberals, and a great many conservatives I might add, don't get. Government can either create a climate where people who do create jobs will want to create them here; or it can create a climate where job creators will go create them elsewhere where they are appreciated.

Job creators are not slaves; we do not have to come here and we do not have to stay here. Most of us have deep roots in this state and would desperately like to stay; that is why we come down on the side of reforming our government institutions and improving our business climate.

Some people will get angry reading this post. Go ahead, cuss all you want, but be sure to tell me how many jobs you have created when you add your comments.

Smokeless

Here's the difference between smoking and being a 'hole: you can quit smoking.

Fresh off their victory over liberty with last year's indoor smoking ban, the fun police have opened a new front in their war on happiness: banning e-cigarettes, those electronic devices people use to inhale and exhale water vapor in place of smoking cigarettes.

That's right, water vapor - the exact same stuff rising up from the steaming cups of vegan chili, fair trade coffee and herbal tea that the know-betters sip while they sit around worrying that the rest of us might have found a way to enjoy ourselves without their permission.

My guess is that they could not agree on what kind of helmet should be required to puff an electronic cigarette, so they just decided to ban them altogether.

It's hard to know what is more offensive to them - that a corporation makes a profit on the things or that conservative radio talk show host Vicki McKenna likes to vape. Maybe they just want people to keep smoking since their beloved government couldn't run a week without tobacco taxes.

The state-wide smoking ban was an outrageous affront to liberty in its own right - people have a right to smoke and people have a right to allow smoking or to ban smoking on their own private property, as they see fit. But at least the cob-up-it crowd could argue about second-hand smoke with only one set of fingers crossed behind their backs.

How is it they can avoid patronizing gay bars and strip clubs yet cannot grasp the notion of simply walking past any joint that puts a two-foot-tall Joe Camel sign right on the front door?

If the next place has a neon pink lung with a smiley face on it, and a barker yelling "no smoke in here" in seven languages, you cruise on in and order up that chardonnay. Seemed like a doable compromise to me, and no, I don't smoke in case you were wondering...

So what is their rationale this time? These new electronic devices do not expose anyone to carcinogens, so that canard is out. They don't stink up the cashmere, so glam up, Barbie and Ken. And they do not affect people with asthma, or allergies, or any other known medical condition, so they can't hide behind wheezing kids again this time.

In fact, the same people who want to ban e-cigs think nothing of holding their own kids' heads under a towel and forcing them to huff on Vicks from a vaporizer for hours on end. But if you take just one little hit on your own personal nic-vaporizor on the far end of the bowling alley – just one - they get their thongs all up in a bunch.

Why? Because you are enjoying yourself doing something they do not approve of – cut through the sanctimonious bullshit and lousy science and that's what this all boils down to. Do-gooders don't care if the things they ban are actually bad for you or not; they ban things to make themselves feel good about themselves. It never was about second-hand smoke; it is second-hand fun that they are afraid of. The attempt to ban e-cigs proves it.

They are addicted to regulating just as surely as the nicotine addict craves his smokes, gum, patch, or vaporizer. In New York, where the first ban on vaping was proposed, advocates argued that since we don't know that there aren't any harmful substances in e-cigs, they must be banned (with government grant money dispensed to study the problem, surprise, surprise).

The more you think about it, the dumber that argument gets – because I don't know A, you can't do B.

Made sense to the Wisconsin Department of Health Services, which issued a release supporting a ban on electronic cigarettes just hours after their ban on for-real smoking went into effect last July. The FDA recently argued for jurisdiction to regulate e-cigs because – and I kid you not – until we study them further, we can't say that there is no tobacco in them. Herman Cain is right – stupid people are ruining this country.

Our Constitution was written to protect individual liberty from the coercive power of the state. Our founders knew that majority rule was mob rule, and they were careful to construct a system where the rights of the minority were not dependent on the whimsy of the majority.

They knew there would always be people whose idea of democracy is a vote on whether to drown witches or burn them.

46 million Americans smoke; I'm not one of them. A few million people use electronic cigarettes; I'm not one of them, either. My duty as a citizen and a patriot is neither to stop them nor to encourage them; my duty as a patriot is to mind my own damn business. And I am one gonzo patriot let me tell you - so vape 'em if you got 'em!

Even if the things are made of medical bio-waste and mustard gas, it's not my place to tell you what you can and cannot put into your own body, although I would sure like to ban the sticks that some people have jammed up their rears.

If you are one of them, please, PLEASE...just put on a helmet and some body armor, loop yourself with bubble wrap, seat belt yourself into a well-padded oxygen chamber with 18 layers of heap filter, and wait for the rapture to come.

And leave the rest of us, who like running with scissors from time to time, alone.

Busybodies

If nothing else, this past month of angry protests have reminded us that "the state" is not an inanimate object or legal abstraction; rather it is the people who write its laws, carry them out, and rule on disputes arising from their implementation.

The farther removed the unit of government, the more distant and impersonal it seems to us. While the states are waging heated personal and partisan budget battles, the Democrats and Republicans in the U.S. Congress agree on 99.4% of federal government spending in the series of continuing resolutions they both laughably describe as their budget "showdown".

Listening to them posture and preen over the paltry 6/10 of 1% in dispute is like watching two morbidly obese dieters haggling over how many sparkly things to pick off the Krispy Kremes before wrapping them in bacon and dropping them in the deep-fryer. It is hard for us to fathom trillions of dollars, let alone to grasp how much unwanted intrusion into our lives is perpetrated by taxing, borrowing, and then spending that many zeros.

But recently Senator Rand Paul personalized it for us, scolding Department of Energy official Kathleen Hogan for promulgating regulations which deny the consumer's right to choose products, and citing appliances, toilets, and light bulbs as examples. While the media focused on the entertaining frustration of Senator Paul, it was her response was the interesting part: she argued that since the enabling legislation had bi-partisan support, the American people *did* make a choice.

Has the collectivist mindset of the politico ever been more perfectly revealed? When 535 individuals in Washington, D.C. vote to limit choices for 310 million other individuals, the political class defines that as a choice. Wow. She said it matter-of-factly with a straight face – the face of limitless government mildly annoyed at having to explain herself to an elected representative of the great unwashed.

There is no singular "American people" and there is no singular "choice"; there are Americans who make choices. The ability to choose is the very definition of liberty; Milton Friedman's seminal

---

work on economic liberty was perfectly titled, "Free To Choose", not "Free To Comply".   Until fairly recently, all Americans believed in liberty as our first principle, regardless of our party loyalty.

Libertarians still do. We reject collectivist socio-economic and political theories of both the left and the right. We recognize the full dignity of the individual, not a diluted proportion derived from membership in a government-designated herd.

We believe the only legitimate purpose of government is to protect our rights and keep us safe – from others, not from ourselves. We acknowledge only individual and universal rights; if a "right' is not universal, or if someone else must be compelled to produce it, then it is a privilege, a reversible legislative whim.

We respect the fundamental right of each individual person to make choices based upon his/her own conscience and beliefs. And we require individuals to own the consequences of their choices. Self-government was once the defining characteristic of the American dream; it is now considered radical, even hateful.

Senator Paul spoke for us when he told the DOE official he was insulted that she would fine us and throw us in jail for no other reason than that we would not share her opinion of what we should buy. It has been years since anyone in Washington has described the offensive nature of busybody government so succinctly.

When she quipped that she could help him find a government-approved toilet that worked, his pitch-perfect response was, "and will you pay for it?"   No answer, face expressionless, unable to comprehend the question.

When he went on to actually refer to the people writing regulations at DOE as "busybodies", Senator Paul was not politically correct, but he was correct.   That remark got him reprimanded by the Chairman of his committee, a fellow Republican, for being too personal in his criticisms of DOE, as if it were the marble floors and the freight elevators at DOE headquarters on Independence Ave. that drew up the regulations in question, not Ms. Hogan and her staff.

But it is not the cubicles that do the coercing in government; it is the people who work in them. Our problem is not what we pay them; it is what we pay them to do. We have given them entirely too much control over our lives; and we have entirely too many of them in entirely too many offices of entirely too many buildings in entirely too many agencies in entirely too many units of government whose overlaps overlap.

Now that we have seen public sector unions use government records to assemble hit-lists of boycott targets in Wisconsin, do you still think Libertarians are overly paranoid about the amount of personal data compiled on us by state workers? Do you now understand the danger of busybody government?

Frank Zappa summed it up nicely when he said, "The most important thing to do in your life is to not interfere in someone else's life."

And what is government but the organized interference into someone else's life? If you think about it, most government employees make their living telling other people what they can and can't do. Ironically, that is what made them come unhinged in Wisconsin when someone finally returned the favor.

Working for the government does not make government workers bad people; it just makes them people doing bad things. It is those things – everything from invading foreign countries, to bailing out banks, to making us buy light bulbs that suck – that have to stop before we can get along again, and before we can even think about getting our fiscal house in order and our economy moving again.

Recipe for a Libertarian

Here's how you make a libertarian: take a Republican, and cut off the war, drug prison, and churchy parts; then you take a Democrat, and cut off the parts that take all of your money and tell you what to do.

Put what's left into a blender while stirring in the Constitution and Austrian School economic theory. Oh, yeah, and guns – don't forget the guns...we really like guns. And gold...if you can't break a tooth on it, it isn't real money.

Anyway, bring the mixture to a boil – any war, financial meltdown, ban, mandate, or picture of Ben Bernanke will get us boiling – and then let simmer for about 2-5 years, reducing to core principles while seasoning to taste. Double the cook times if educated in a public school after 1985.

Voila! There is your recipe for making a Libertarian; it only makes a single serving, because no two of us will come out exactly the same, which makes the perfect-purity sort of libertarians vibrate in place, but it makes the rest of us happy and our discussions interesting.

It is that season-to-taste step that is most crucial; add more civil liberties, or spoon in a few extra scoops of capitalism, a dash of conspiracy here and there, cut back from legalized dope to medical marijuana, pour in some "green" food coloring, or even substitute ingredients – pro-life libertarians have done that. No need to add nuts, we have plenty already, thank you very much.

Making a libertarian is quite a bit more difficult than creating another Democrat or Republican. Democrat is more of a birth-demographic designation than any particular political philosophy, except for that part about taking all your money and telling you what to do. And most Republicans I know found their compass by asking the deep and probing question, "Dad, what are we?" Libertarians had to think our way here.

Libertarians don't do big rallies and demonstrations; we don't have the numbers or the coercion skills to pull it off. Besides, the argument for eliminating fractional reserve banking, privatizing currency, and ending the Fed would be a four-page sign in 12 pt font that you would have to sit down to read in good light. USA Today prefers pictures of angry people yelling.

We don't chant well, either: "Hey, hey...ho, ho...liberty is the absence of government in choice...and government is the absence of liberty in choice...and...um...tyranny is the absence of choice in government!" Or, "No Justice, No Peace...peace being the abolishment of any form of government-sanctioned coercive force against persons or property with the intent to diminish individual volition!" It just sounds like mumbling, and the megaphone batteries run out before we ever make it all the way to the end.

And we don't have any solid-gold protest songs to sing, either; the Canadian power trio Rush is the most famous Libertarian band, but none of us actually know all the words to "Freewill". Plus, you have to totally concentrate to clap to the changing rhythms of a Rush song. It's not like "We Shall Overcome", where you just sing the title three times and then add..."someday". Cripes, there are only four notes; you could be Schlitz-face wasted and still make your difference. Those were the days.

So we Libertarians pretty much just glob on to somebody else's gig. I look like a Republican, so they let me do tea parties with them sometimes. If I showed up on Mifflin Street, people would think I'm DEA, so we send other libertarians who blend in a little better. The greenies like anyone with a beard, the anti-war folks love our hippies, and we have some women who can fit in anywhere – think Birkenstocks, leather, and open carry. Mind-bending, they are.

I think a lot of people are libertarians and just don't know it yet. Are you conservative on economic issues, neutral on the social stuff, and non-interventionist in foreign affairs? Are you a FLIP person – free trade, limited government, individual liberty, and private property? When you hear "bi-partisan" do you think you are about to get screwed twice? You might just be one of us.

In the weeks ahead, many libertarian organizations will be having their annual state conventions, which will feature speakers, information, networking, and social hours. Campaign

4 Liberty, Libertarian Party, Republican Liberty Caucus, and Liberty On The Rocks are all good places to meet like-minded people, learn more about libertarian themes, and have fun. Consider this my annual plug to check 'em out.

They all have websites and Facebook pages with their event schedules and locations – Wisconsin's LP convention is April 1&2 at Olympia Resort in Oconomowoc and if there was ever a patriot family business deserving our support, my friends Rick and Rudy Eckert at Olympia are top of the charts.

And about that churchy part - I didn't mean throw it away, just keep it out of reach of the fools that run government. The separation of church and state is not for the benefit of the state; it is for the preservation of the church. Our rights are an endowment from our Creator, and we don't share our birthright with the help.

And have fun. Our Declaration of Independence did not say life, liberty, and the pursuit of somber obligatory duty. It said happiness, and that is my sincere wish for all who follow this column and share it with their friends. Be happy.

CAPITALISTA!

Working Man

Of all of the myths that persist about wealth and work, perhaps the most stubborn is the myth of the working man; the stoic character who toils harder, grinds longer, contributes more, and is paid less than his presumptively non-working overlords.

Socialists, liberals, and Democrats claim to be "for" the working man – as long as it's the union-represented working man. Capitalists, conservatives, and Republicans also claim to be "for" the working man, too – mostly they mean the tax-paying working man who owns a small business. Both claim the other Party is out to stick it to the working man, and both claim to be the working man's only salvation.

Get real. Republicans and Democrats don't care a dollop about the working man, the working woman, the working baby, the working mule, or the working space-alien. They care about votes; enough votes to win elections and secure political power. That is *all* they care about, and it is somewhere between incredibly naïve and completely delusional to think otherwise.

How about we start with dropping the class-warfare bullsnot; it is boring and tedious and this is not Germany in 1848. Do you think wealthy people don't work? How do you think they got that way, or stay there? Why does Tiger Woods make tens of millions when the pro at the city course makes $50 grand? Because Tiger Woods works his ass off, hitting the practice range, hitting the weight room, hitting on barmaids...ok, that was uncalled for...but you see the point.

Tiger Woods doesn't get paid millions because he is Tiger Woods; he gets paid millions because he *plays* like Tiger Woods. And he plays like Tiger Woods because he has worked at it harder and longer than the guy who plays like John Daly. Ditto Oprah, Bill Gates, villains-du-jure Koch brothers, Al Gore, and the millions of business owners who earn more than me because they produce more – more of the things that people want to buy. Don't hate them, thank them.

I don't generally talk about my own employer in my blogs and speeches, but I will share this observation from over 35 years in business: the working men (and women) who come in early, stay late, work on weekends, travel on their own time, and take on the toughest assignments are generally the highest-paid employees in the firm. As well as young people who will be the highest paid employees in the firm someday.

We do not work harder because we get paid more; we get paid more because we work harder. Not just work harder, but accomplish more; ultimately our earnings are determined by the value we add. Today is a Saturday, and the other folks who I saw in the office today were all upper-charts. This is pretty typical.

Several years ago I looked around at a meeting of our company's executive team and here is what I saw: a pastor's kid, a miner's kid, a bartender's kid, a laborer's kid, two factory worker's kids, an accountant's kid, an air force brat.

Not a single silver spoon around that big mahogany boardroom table. In my experience, this is the rule, not the exception – it is what makes America such a unique and great country. Upward mobility is the defining characteristic of capitalism, and the thing that socialists destroy along the way to making everyone equally mediocre.

When I was young and dumb and poor, I was jealous of the executives that had company cars and reserved parking spots with their names on them. One Saturday, as I was working a little OT on my $1.15/hour stockroom job and feeling sorry for myself, I noticed that the only other cars in the parking lot were the ones in the reserved places.

When I asked one of those executives what it took to get to his station in life, he answered, "you are already doing it." That was the Saturday I decided to quit being dumb and poor; and yes, those are choices. The young part, sadly, is not.

Salomon Wilcots, the NFL football analyst and former player, put it this way to a caller on his radio program who complained about the unfairness of high salaries of football players compared to the wages of others who do physically demanding work: "If you want what I have, then go do what I did." In case anyone wonders, here is what I did:

CAPITALISTA!

I got a second job, I went back to school, I took assignments and promotions that no one else wanted, I changed fields, I earned professional credentials, I changed employers and moved, I married once and married right, I learned to treat employees with respect, I was a volunteer firefighter, I changed fields again, I changed employers and moved again, I went back to school again, I got involved in charities and community organizations, I quit all my favorite self-destructive habits, I went back to school again, I mentored kids, I joined university boards and advised minority business associations, I moved two more times on transfers, I got active in politics, I ran for Congress, I started writing, and I still work more hours at 57 than 98% of the 27 year-old fast-trackers gunning for my job who will read this article. Not that it matters, but I have two ADA-qualifying disabilities, and I am not even the smartest guy in my family, let alone the world. Point being - I am not special.

So you know what I have to say to those who call me a greedy fat cat corporatist that doesn't care about the working man? Screw you. I *am* a working man.

And here is some unsolicited advice: stay dumb and poor and bitter – it suits you. Wait around like some helpless kitten with its eyes shut tight and its mouth wide open hoping that a teat will appear from nowhere to keep it alive. Pray to your union to save you, or your Democrats to hug you, or your Republicans to liberate you. Stomp your feet, hold your breath, and covet, covet, covet. That is the path to success your leaders have laid out for you, so follow it blindly despite what you see plainly with your own eyes.

But enjoy your journey without me, friend, because I don't have any more time to waste on you – I work. There are thousands of hard-working employees and family members who depend on me, tens of thousands more in the communities where we work and live who would suffer if we fail. Those are the people I care about, and that is a full time job, sorry.

And don't you dare lecture me about the hard-working public servants in this state as if they were the only ones who ever put in a full shift. While my cane and I are knee deep in the mud of an underground mine in the Andes trying to sell equipment to keep our hard-working Wisconsin factories running, the trains up to Machu Pichu are packed with professors on sabbatical and public pensioners in their 50's spilling pisco sours on their Birkenstocks. Talk to the hand.

Private sector workers produce all of the wealth that we share in this great nation. 93% of them have chosen to work free of union impairment. Those are the working people I care about; them and their children. And I care about them deeply; enough to fight for their right to discover for themselves how high is up for them.

Middle Class

The left continues to prattle on and on about the "war on the middle class", which is the label they attach nowadays to any serious discussion of government spending.

For the moment, let's put aside the rather obvious point that the middle class will be the first to be wiped out if the grown-ups don't avert the debt-induced economic collapse and currency debasement that looms. Instead, let's visit a country where the pro-labor policies our American unionists demand have already been in place for 80 years.

This nation's Federal Labor Law was enacted in 1932. It sets not only basic minimum wage, but a different minimum wage for each general category of employment, flexed upwards to account for education and regional cost of living disparities. Salaries must be increased annually at a minimum set by law. *Take that, Scott Walker!*

For every six days of work, employees get one paid day of rest. Overtime at double pay must be paid for exceeding any 8 hour shift, not just a weekly total. No one can work more than 9 hours of overtime in a week. *Screw you, Chris Christie!*

Every worker is guaranteed a minimum of 6 days of vacation when hired, and 2 days are added for each year worked up to five. Employees get 25% premium added to their pay while on vacation. 7 mandatory holidays, with triple time pays if worked. *How do you like me now, Jerry Brown, you hippie traitor!*

There is mandatory severance pay for both termination and resignation – three months plus additional 20 days for each year employed. And the fired employee is entitled to sue for reinstatement at the employer's expense; the law presumes wrongful termination unless the employer can prove otherwise. *Talk to the clenched fist, Rand Paul!*

Employers must fund employees' personal retirement accounts, as well as provide housing allowance, annual bonus, government health care contributions, and other benefits totaling 29% of base salary. Plus profit sharing at 10% of earnings must be paid to workers, with management excluded. *Eat it, lousy Koch Brothers!*

Labor unions must be recognized if just 20% of the workforce registers. Collective bargaining agreements are negotiated between the employer's representative and the representative of the national union every two years. *Holy Card Check, Batman, only 20%? Wait until the other occasional dishwashers hear about this...*

The entrenched national unions all back one political party, a democrat-socialist party which has held serve for 72 of the 80 years since these pro-labor laws were enacted. The politicians are pro-union, the judges are pro-union, the government is pro-union and the law itself is pro-union. *Dude, where's my passport?*

Can you guess this land of union plenty and middle-class abundance? Mexico.

Yes, *that* Mexico. So when you see all those public union workers protesting in American state capitals, here is the translation of their war-chant: "hey, hey, ho, ho, let's be just like Mex-i-co!"

After 80 years of the unionist stacked-deck, oil-rich Mexico's nominal per-capita GDP is $9,423 ranking it 64th, just behind rioting-as-we-speak Libya and economic juggernaut Uruguay. Eight decades of living the union dream has produced a living standard less than 1/5 of its union-busting, worker-be-damned Gringo neighbor to the north. Much worse, actually, because $25 billion of Mexico's income is remittances sent home from the millions of Mexicans working union-free in the United States.

The richest man in the world is Mexican, while 40% of his countrymen live in poverty. Mexico's income gap is greater than ours; so too its urban/rural disparity. Mexico's middle class – and this is all about the middle class, remember - is ¼ the size of ours, proportional to population.

So why haven't 80 years of union privilege, strict labor laws, single party rule, and mandated wealth redistribution brought prosperity to Mexico? For the same reason they won't here and have anywhere else ever - you can't redistribute skill.

Celine Dion is wealthy because she has a beautiful voice and has worked insanely hard her whole life to perfect her act. While the state can force her to share her earnings with me, it can't make that sound come out of my mouth.

For me to get paid more than my singing is worth, she must be paid less than hers is worth. That is the simple arithmetic of socialism; and it works the same for masons, teachers, engineers, accountants, plumbers, store clerks, managers, and machinists, too.

And what does Ms. Dion do when she is paid less than she is worth? She quits singing, and we both get poorer. Figuratively speaking, Mexico's 80 years of pro-labor, anti-business politics has created a land of bad singers; ditto for Greece, Detroit and the Milwaukee Public School district, where even the Principals are unionized.

If tough labor laws, pro-union government, and wealth redistribution were the pathway to prosperity, then it would be Mexico building that wall on our southern border, not us.

Skills, not union propaganda, are the pathway to the middle class, and it's too bad our children are getting only the latter in the classroom these days.

Shores of Tripoli

Here is the difference between President Obama and his predecessor George W. Bush: President Obama does not just do bad things, he does bad things badly.

It's not just that starting up our third undeclared war of regime change in the Muslim world is foolish; it is the way the President did it that disturbs. In the second half of his term, it is not unreasonable to expect our President to have a clue.

First of all, we should never send our troops to battle because the United Nations tells us to, or even asks us to. We don't work for them. The United States' vital security interests are exclusively ours to define and defend. The Constitution only prescribes one legal means to start a war – by declaration of Congress. That would be our Congress, Mr. President.

Second, if the Arab League is convinced that a no-fly zone was needed to contain Colonel Kaddafi, they are perfectly capable of executing that maneuver themselves. We have given billions upon billions in military aid, aircraft, training, and logistical support to the Egyptians, Saudi's, Kuwaiti's and Jordanians. Libya is their neighborhood, he is their neighbor, and this is their problem. It's not ours.

Third, if the situation in Libya is important enough to go to war, it is important enough to cancel a junket to Rio to run the bloody thing. Commander-in-Chief is not a title of nobility, it is a job description; it is a high honor, not an inconvenience, to command our troops. Those troops are at risk and people are being killed in Benghazi and Tripoli while our President is down congratulating the Brazilians for drilling offshore? Absurdity beats irony in triple overtime.

What kind of Fire Chief would send his best battalions in to fight a raging inferno that threatens to engulf the whole downtown, and then trundle off to Mardi Gras with the missus? Our war fighters have only one purpose, and it is not to run errands for the U.N., the Arab League, or France. It is to defend the United States of America in declared wars. Has Libya attacked? Has war been declared? I didn't think so.

Three days into the Teleprompter President's war on Libya, NATO forces threatened to withdraw in a squabble over who is in charge of the operations. I am not an expert in such things, but it seems to me prudent to have those disagreements away from the cameras and microphones, and perhaps *before* we started lobbing cruise missiles, B-52's, and F-18s at targets surrounded by human shields.

And a State Department official apparently told a CNN reporter that our targeting is not very good because our intelligence is not very good and we don't have good ties to the people we are assisting. Do these people understand that they get TV and internet in Libya? Again, not my area of expertise, but it does not take a degree from Army War College to know that you shouldn't announce to your enemy that you don't know squat. He will figure that out on his own soon enough.

President Obama is a black George W. Bush channeling Jimmy Cater, only less competent than either one. Did his speech announcing the Libyan operations not parrot George W. Bush's justifications for Afghan and Iraqi interventions? Did his fighter plane crashing in the desert not bring back humiliating memories of helicopters going down when Carter botched the Iranian hostage rescue?

The anti-war left's defense of this guy is both astonishing and appalling. Howard Dean, whose 2004 Presidential bid rested squarely on opposition to George W. Bush's undeclared wars, now defends President Obama's expansion of those two and his opening of a third in Libya. The whole bogus movement was never anti-war; it is anti-Republican, just too smugly sanctimonious to admit it. And too busy now protesting for public union privileges to be bothered with such trivia as another war ordered up like room service by their guy.

And Republican leadership is not exactly bronze statue material over the question of Libya. Speaker Boehner "has questions". Really - like what kind of questions? Ron Paul doesn't have questions; Rand Paul doesn't have questions; Justin Amash doesn't have questions; the Republican Liberty Caucus doesn't have questions. All came out immediately against the unauthorized use of force to oust Kaddafi.

Newt Gingrich calls for even more aggressive military action, because "now is a good time", to remove a dictator we don't care much for. Sarah Palin called for a no-fly zone 3 weeks before President Obama came around to the idea. Snobby Palin bashers might want to cut her some slack, considering that You-Betcha Barbie got to their guy's answer on her own three weeks quicker than he did with his crackerjack team of advisors.

Like Bill Clinton's transparently shameless missile attacks on Baghdad during his impeachment proceedings, President Obama's war against Kaddafi conveniently pushed his $2 trillion lie about the debt in his sham budget to the back burners. Nobody is reading CBO reports when there is live feed of crying women on CNN. And the Supreme Court rejected the Federal Reserve's appeal, so now the Fed will have to tell us who they gave out $9 trillion to during the banking crisis. Expect a heavy bombardment on the day that list is released.

Doing bad things badly; that is President Obama's modus operandi. When he nationalized banks and automobile companies he did a bad thing badly. His economic stimulus was a bad thing done badly. The President's Heath Care deform was a bad thing done badly. His drilling ban was a bad thing done badly. His financial reforms were a bad thing done badly. His EPA carbon dioxide regulating is a bad thing done badly. His budget is a bad thing done badly. The list is too long to recount here.

And now he has started a third war of choice in the Middle East – another bad thing done badly. And if the President's criteria for war is now any loudmouth SOB who is mean to his people and not friendly to us, he has about 50 more of these bastards to take down before we show him the door in our peaceful method of regime change, the ballot box.

And then can hang out in Rio as often and as long as his little heart desires.

Zen Capitalist

It must be difficult to go through life as a socialist.

When every disparity is an injustice, then every human being you encounter is either your oppressor or your victim, depending on their wealth relative to yours. Those with more incite hatred, and those with less induce guilt.

Hatred and guilt do not move others to cooperate, so socialists must rely on coercion to co-exist. Coercion, hatred, and guilt – there is a recipe for an unhappy life.

How much better it is to live as a capitalist free-trader.

When every other human on the planet is a potential partner in mutually beneficial exchange, then each encounter begins with hope and anticipation, and ends in gratitude - the thank-you, thank-you ritual of purchase that we all know so well.

Volition cannot be coerced; so persuasion is the means by which capitalists co-exist. Hope, persuasion, and gratitude – no wonder we are so pleasant and good-natured; and no wonder those miserable socialists are insanely jealous.

It is a choice to be socialist or capitalist; it is not a genetic assignment, like race, gender, hair color, dominant hand, or sexual preference. Each of us is free to choose the basis for our interaction with the rest of humanity - either the hatred-guilt-coercion paradigm, or the hope-gratitude-persuasion paradigm, or some watered-down variant of the two extremes.

Socialists are not miserable because they are poor; a great many of them live in the cocoon of security and privilege known as government work. Even our millionaire socialists, like Michael Moore and Nancy Pelosi, and our billionaire socialists like George Soros, appear to spend nearly every waking hour pissed off that someone somewhere has more money than they do. How awful for them.

Young people, listen to me: if it bothers you that someone else has more than you do, the problem is yours, not theirs. There

---

are billions of people in this world, and you will always be able to point to someone who has more and to someone who has less. It is up to you decide when you will quit pointing in anger and start living in serenity.

Capitalists, as a general rule, do not covet. We admire the wealth created by others, but we do not imagine it is rightfully ours. Socialists need capitalists to produce the wealth they redistribute, while capitalists do not need socialists for anything. It is this unequal and fundamentally parasitic relationship that drives socialists to acts of disproportionate hysteria at the slightest hint of abandonment.

Recall that Wisconsin's public sector unions accepted benefit concessions readily, if not happily. It was only the prospect of having to collect dues from their own members – to survive by consent - that brought out the drums, death threats, vandalism, extortion, boycotts, harassment, intimidation, fraud, and angry protests.

All you need to know about compulsory unionism is the compulsory part. And compulsory unionism is socialism practiced at the level of the firm.

And what is moral about taking someone else's money to buy the things you wish not to pay for yourself? Should you buy my health care, food, and train fare so that I can use my money to get a Captain Morgan tattoo on spring break?

The first responsibility we have to our fellow man is to not be a burden; to be economically autonomous. Charity is only possible from surplus; you can't be your brother's keeper if you both need to be kept.

Are libertarian capitalists uncharitable because we oppose all forms of government assistance – programs funded by confiscatory taxation and run for the benefit of the public unions who administer them? I'll tell you what is uncharitable: incompetence, deceit, false hope, ignorance, and economic suicide.

The greatest threat to the Western democracies is not Al Qaeda; it is our unsustainable public debt and the impending collapse of our currencies. The welfare/warfare state is devouring itself to keep up the appearance of sustaining commitments it cannot possibly keep.

Capitalists did not deliver us here to the edge of the abyss; it is the enemies of capitalism who argue for deficit spending and monetizing the debt. For 100 years, the socialists' answer to every problem has been more government. They have created a beast so large and slow it cannot save itself from itself.

The capitalist knows what the socialist will never learn; redistribution destroys wealth, while voluntary exchange creates it. We prospered as a nation when we held liberty as our first principle and embraced capitalism as the only system compatible with our notions of self-sovereignty, equality, and freedom.

True prosperity will not return until we do so again.

Bonus Selection: OWN IT

Author's Note: Soon after the draft of this book was compiled, I published an essay entitled "Own It".

There was a taxpayer rally announced for the Wisconsin Capitol on Saturday, April 16, 2011. A coalition of liberal and union activist groups organized to suppress the free speech rights of the taxpayer/tea party by intimidation, disruption, and noisemaking.

I was on a business trip in Latin America, but watched internet feeds, twitter threads, youTube postings, and facebook newsfeeds of the day's events. I was disgusted and appalled by what I saw. I wrote "Own It" in about 15 minutes; it is a call for decent Democrats to disown the tactics of their ends-justifies-means leaders or leave the Party.

I guess it was pretty good. The social networks shared and reposted and retweeted and all that stuff that I don't understand. Vicki McKenna did not only share the links with her fans, she read it in its entirety over the air.

A fan, Lori Lang, created a phenomenal graphic and made it available for those who wanted OWN IT t-shirts, mugs, stickers, etc. A line from the piece, "I don't speak drum" took on a life of its own.

I have received thousands of favorable comments, only a handful of negative ones, and a surprising number of Democrats who let me know that my essay triggered them to reexamine their affiliation with the party they had spent a lifetime supporting.

That is why I write; to make people think for themselves and form convictions that they can own.

CAPITALISTA!

Own It

Although I am not a Democrat or a Republican, I used to understand why other people would choose to be one or the other. And I can still understand how some people can be Republicans, but it is beyond my comprehension how anyone could still be a Democrat in Wisconsin in the age of YouTube.

The Democrats' response to losing an election here has been appalling; disgraceful conduct documented with phone cameras for the whole world to see. Democrat rallies and protests have been marked by profanity, intimidation, death threats, vandalism, trespassing on private residences, anti-American rhetoric, boycotts of neutral businesses, extortion, and fraud.

My dear Democrat friends, that is not what democracy looks like; it is what *Democrats* look like. Your Party has become vile, disgraceful, and disgusting, and you have lived long enough in denial of what and who you have become. Own it.

It's not just the mob scenes that disgust. Perhaps the most dishonest political ad in history was run by Democrats in a supposedly non-partisan Supreme Court race, exploiting the victim of child abuse for political gain. Own it, Party of the children.

Your Democrat legislators wore union t-shirts on the floor of the assembly while in session; shouting and throwing things and threatening to kill a female Republican lawmaker. This is how you treat women who think for themselves. Own it, Party of women.

Your public sector unions – firefighters and teachers - organized a campaign to drown out yesterday's taxpayer rally on the steps of the Capitol building. You exist now only to deprive others of their right to be heard; and your idea of civil is dropping F-bombs at a child who came to hear Sarah Palin speak. You have embraced disgrace – so own it, Party of civil rights.

You booed the national anthem. Read that again, friends; take a moment to reflect fully upon the depths to which your Democrat party has sunk, and then OWN IT.

On that same day the office of a recall drive against one of the 14 AWOL Democrat Senators was burglarized with computers and petitions stolen – just like Nixon in 1972. You also threatened to blow up a radio station over content you don't like. You were busy little fascist criminals on Saturday - own it, Nixonites .

If these are just isolated examples of people acting out, then show me where your Party leaders have denounced them. Who have you expelled from your Party for the shame they have brought to it? And who is your Ron Paul, your conscience who calls you out when you have strayed from your core values - Charlie Rangel?

Your Democrat State Senator Lena Taylor recently got herself on TV to rant against some $142 million of tax breaks Governor Walker has given to his cronies, but when asked, she could not name one. Your comprehensive plan to balance the budget and avoid default is to chant "Fox Lies!" This is the depth or your intellectual curiosity and the extent of your economic literacy. Own it.

Yours is the party that extended our military stay in Iraq, increased our commitment in Afghanistan, spread that war into Pakistan and Yemen, and started another in Libya. When it was Bush dropping the bombs, you came to us Libertarians and begged us to join you to stop him; haven't seen you around now that is your guy killing little brown people. He lies to you and you love him for it. Own that.

What does it take for you decent Democrats - and I know there are many of you who will read this - to walk away from a Party that has already abandoned the principles that attracted you to it in the first place? How much of your pride are you still willing to forfeit to a Party that has none? What is your last straw – does blowing an angry horn at a downs-syndrome person for waving a flag not do it for you?

Disown it or own it – which is it?

It's your mirror you need to look in every day, not mine. It was a far less obnoxious abandonment of principle that led me to leave the GOP many years ago. It is true that I get along better with them than with Democrats as a rule; that rule is that they don't send me death threats when I write something they don't like.

Nearly a third of the American electorate is now non-affiliated with either of the two major Parties; each Democrat/socialist/union rally drives more of you into our camp.

You Democrats do not persuade us with temper tantrums, threats, profane personal attacks, and all manner of judicial chicanery. I don't even know what you stand for anymore; I don't speak drum.

Yours was once the Party of Kennedy; it is now the Party that boos the national anthem. Own that – and then walk away. You will feel better about yourself, and you might just save your Party from the hooligans who have run it into disrepute.

ABOUT THE AUTHOR

Tim Nerenz is an international business executive with over 35 years of experience manufacturing American products and exporting them all over the world.

Tim did his undergraduate work at Carthage College in Kenosha, Wisconsin, and went back to school later in life to earn AGDM and MBA degrees from Athabasca University in Alberta, Canada and a Ph.D. in Business Administration from Northcentral University in Prescott, Arizona.

One of the longest-serving members of Athabasca University's Governing Council, Tim helped establish an alliance of North American distance education pioneers - Athabasca University, Technologico Monterrey, and University of Maryland University College. For his service, Dr. Nerenz was inducted into the Order of Athabasca University in 2011.

In 2010, Tim ran for the U.S. House of Representatives as the Libertarian Party candidate in Wisconsin's second district (Madison), but was forced to withdraw from the race when he and his wife Joanne relocated.

His campaign stump speech introduction - I want to be your Congressman, not your mommy - foreshadowed the direct style and sense of humor that delights fans of *Dr. Tim's Moment of Clarity*, the blog that survived the campaign.

You can follow Dr. Tim's Moment of Clarity and buy Tim's books at his website www.timnerenz.com.

ompliance

9 6 8 7 7 *